MAZAMA
The Past 125 Years

Doug Devin

Published 2008 by the Shafer Historical Museum, Winthrop, Washington
978-0-9779726-3-0   Devin, Doug. *Mazama: The Past 125 Years.*
                 Winthrop, Washington: Shafer Historical Museum, 2008.

Text by Doug Devin
Edited by Karen West
Design by Sally Ranzau

Printed in the USA

Front cover photographs:
The Mazama Goat designed by Mary Sharman for the Mazama Country Store is owned by Missy and Rick LeDuc and used with their permission.

The classic Roy Kumm barn that housed a dairy herd at one time. (Doug Devin)

Traffic at the Mazama junction of Lost River Road and Goat Creek Road in the 1930s. (Greydon Patterson)

The Angus McLeod building in Mazama served as a hotel, saloon, store, post office and community gathering place for many years. The only identification found with this undated photograph was Mr. McLeod, far left, and Dad Callahan, third from left. (Okanogan County Historical Society)

Back cover photograph:
Skiers in the Early Winters area in the late 1920s. From front to back, Shirley Grant, Wayne Grant, Bud Short and Earl Short. The Grant and Short families were neighbors. (Bud Short)

ACKNOWLEDGEMENTS

The Shafer Historical Museum Board of Directors wishes to thank Doug Devin for the gift of his manuscript copyright and the anonymous donor whose generous grant helped defray printing costs. The museum will receive all proceeds from the sale of this book.

DEDICATION

To all the men and women past and present who have given Mazama
its character for today and direction for tomorrow.

INTRODUCTION

I self-published the first edition of this book in the summer of 1997 and ordered a second printing the following fall. The book sold out and has been out of print for a decade. During that time, a number of people have come forward with additional information and corrections to the earlier work. And there have been many changes in Mazama. So when the board of the Shafer Historical Museum expressed an interest in publishing a revised and expanded version of the book, I was happy to contribute my original manuscript and to add material for this edition.

Karen West, a member of the museum board and a retired Seattle Times editor, was the key to getting the project moving and completed. Her experience and editorial skills, together with the museum board members who arranged financing, made the difference between "That's a good idea" and this book. Thus you are holding a completely revised and updated edition of *Mazama The Past 100 Years*, which is now *Mazama The Past 125 Years.*

This history is of the land west of Winthrop, Washington, and east of the Cascade Mountains. Words and photographs hardly begin to do justice to its beauty and majesty. The mountains, valleys, rivers and streams comprise a breathtaking panorama that cannot be adequately described.

The area known today as Mazama (pronounced like Alabama by old-time locals) had other names in earlier times and those are used where appropriate in the text.

Because the histories of Winthrop and the Slate Creek Mining District in the mountains beyond Mazama are recorded in a number of other publications, they are mentioned here only to give context or to note their effects on development of the upper Methow Valley.

Researching the history of an area like Mazama is a fascinating and never-ending endeavor. There is always one more person to interview and another lead to pursue. At some point, I found it necessary to stop gathering and start assembling the material I had collected.

The book is divided into two parts. Part I, "On The Road to Mazama," begins in Winthrop and discusses points of interest along the road all the way to Lost River. Longtime residents Bill and Martha Stewart and Roy and Doris Kumm provided most of the information for Part I. The Stewarts and Roy Kumm are gone now; Doris Kumm is living at Harmony House in Brewster. But their contributions will never be forgotten and their stories are preserved on tape recordings.

Part II, "A Chronological Account of Development in the Mazama Area," starts in the late 1800s. It discusses specific individuals and families, how they came to settle where they did, and their activities and contributions to the emerging community.

Chapters covering recent decades at Early Winters contain more detail than other chapters for several reasons. First, I was intimately involved with the dream of developing a downhill ski area. Secondly, the ski plans brought significant change, especially to the upper valley, and created contentious issues that drew national attention. And finally, the Early Winters project sparked legal challenges that went all the way to the state and U.S.

supreme courts and set precedents regarding water rights and environmental impact procedures that have affected development of other rural properties in the West.

The book's final chapter, "Mazama Enters A New Century," describes the outcome of the Early Winters resort battle and introduces people typical of those arriving as the community continues to change.

Throughout the book I've attempted to capture snapshots of life during each decade, from the time the first white people arrived through the turn of the 21st century, by introducing some of the people who've settled in Mazama.

While I first came here in the 1950s, I didn't move here full time until the late 1970s. I felt there were many people better qualified than I to write this history. However, my many attempts over the years at persuading some of the early settlers to record their recollections were unsuccessful. Thus, I resorted to collecting some of their stories myself, hoping to generate the interest of an experienced author. That didn't work either, so I became a reluctant author by default. I apologize for any omissions and errors, and hope that readers will point them out so that any future editions of this book can be corrected.

I wrote this book so all of us who live in and love the Methow Valley will know that this history is preserved for future generations. The non-profit Shafer Historical Museum will receive all proceeds from its sale.

Doug Devin
Mazama, Washington 2008

HOMESTEADING
THE BEGINNING OF DEVELOPMENT

The United States Congress passed an Act on May 20, 1862, "To Secure Homesteads to Actual Settlers on the Public Domain." Filings were made at the nearest land office, which at that time for Okanogan and the Methow was in Waterville. After the claimed homestead was improved, the president of the United States granted to "said claimant, the tract of land described TO HAVE AND TO HOLD."

The Methow Valley was Indian land until it was opened to white settlement in 1886. By then, much of the West already had been claimed. However, on June 11, 1906, the Homestead Entry Surveys Act was passed to provide a way for settlers to acquire title to public land in federal Forest Reserves that was better suited for agriculture than forestry. Most of the land in Mazama was national forest land at that time.

Thus, all the homestead claims in the Mazama area were made under the 1906 HES Act. To this day descriptions of the land contain references to an HES number and county tax parcels often carry that number as identification. Many of the parcels discussed in this book are referred to by HES number.

Because most of the land had not been surveyed, claims were filed using descriptions and measurements based on witness trees, rocks, rivers and streams. These old surveys were amazingly accurate and the descriptions continued to be used later when the land was sold or divided.

This 1970s aerial photograph looking west shows the upper Methow Valley between Little Boulder Creek on the left and Cedar and Early Winters creeks on the right. The road between Highway 20 and Lost River Road, which crosses the Methow River and leads to the commercial area of Mazama, is at the bottom center. The large forested mountain in the center is Sandy Butte, site of a proposed downhill ski area that created controversy for decades starting in 1970. The rugged, snowy peak behind the butte is Mt. Gardner.

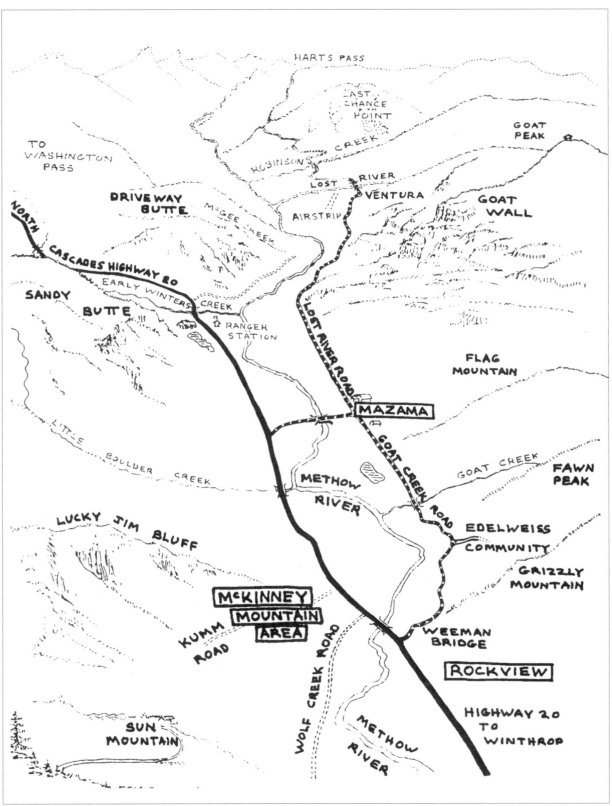

This illustration by Eric Burr identifies the important areas of both early and current Mazama.

PART I
On the Road to Mazama

To gather information about the people who settled the Mazama area, I took two leisurely drives from Winthrop to Lost River in 1990-91. On one occasion I was accompanied by Bill and Martha Stewart. Martha came to the Methow Valley in 1902 as a young girl. Her parents, Tom and Nancy Sloane, homesteaded on HES 200 and 202 in Mazama. The second drive was with Roy and Doris Kumm. Roy's dad, Frank Kumm, was an early settler in the McKinney Mountain area and spent most of his life near Mazama.

On both trips I took notes and tape-recorded the comments of my passengers. The Stewarts and Kumms passed on their knowledge of who lived in which house, who farmed which land and who sold and bought which plots. Their commentary was sprinkled with amusing anecdotes from the early days and the drives brought back memories and stories long forgotten.

What follows in this section is largely based on the Stewarts' and Kumms' stories, often in their own words shared as we drove along the road. Material from additional sources is included.

Bill and Martha Stewart in 1992

Roy and Doris Kumm in 1993

A horse and buggy crosses the Three Mile Bridge over the West Fork of the Methow River near its confluence with Wolf Creek. The bridge was destroyed by the flood of 1894 and later rebuilt as a pedestrian crossing.

Winthrop to Weeman Bridge

In the old days as the road left Winthrop heading west, it wandered around the foot of the hills. About one mile out of town on the left, there was a farm in the big field. The identity of the homesteader is lost to us, but an early owner of the farm was a man named Clark who had lived in the eastern United States. Clark may have been a friend of Guy Waring, who arrived in the Methow Valley in 1891 and started a store in a log cabin. Waring's first wife's maiden name was Clark, so perhaps he was a relative. The Edson family leased the property from Clark and put up lots of hay. Their house and barn were near the present road.

There was another house on the land, down by the Methow River, that was leased by O.K. Gullion, who farmed the upper portion. The field was flood irrigated until the 1948 flood washed out the ditch. The field eventually went to barnaby (knapweed). The remodeled house is still there.

Don Dagnon returned the field to production with the installation of a sprinkler system in the mid-1980s. But in 1993, following the breakup of his marriage, the farm was divided into large tracts and sold by a developer. Several parcels continue to be irrigated and farmed.

On the north side another Clark, Gale Clark, had a house on the bench above the road and did dryland farming.

A fellow by the name of Levi Hicks, who Bill Stewart claimed spent most of his time making moonshine, lived down by the river near here.

The road ran over the hill in those days, past the J.W. Goudy place, which now is the east end of Harold and Tina Heath's Big Valley Ranch. The Goudy house and barn sat up on the hill near an apple tree. To get to the site now you'd have to follow the road that goes to the gravel pit.

WINTHROP TO BOESEL CANYON

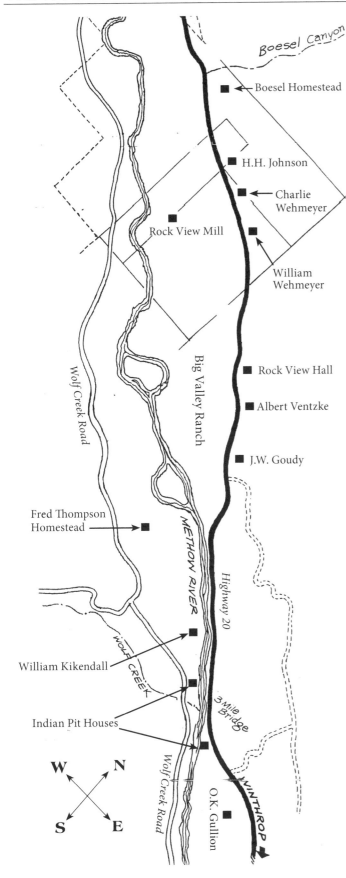

The Thompson place, one of the oldest homesteads in the area, sat across the river near Wolf Creek. Fred Thompson arrived in 1888; his brother George came later. Fred claimed his land because it was free of trees. But as it turned out, the land sat on a pile of rocks, which explained the absence of trees.

William Kikendall had a house next to Thompson, but most of his property was on the hill across the river next to Goudy.

The Indians had a number of pit houses on the Kikendall property and on the west side of the river. The holes still exist and several have been excavated. There are numerous stories recalling that a large number of Indians were in this area. The number of pit house sites, arrowheads and artifacts found nearby give them credence. There is also a story that says a battle between Indians was fought on the flat land where Wolf Creek flows into the Methow River and that after that battle no Indian would pass through that spot after dark.

The Three Mile Bridge, near the confluence of Wolf Creek and the Methow River, was a major river crossing for years.

S. Virginia Moore owned land near where the Heaths live today. Her place was near the pond, then known as Moore's Slough. Before her marriage to John Moore, S. Virginia was Sally Shipp, an artist who grew up as a Chicago society girl. (Her land later became part of Harold Heath's Big Valley Ranch.)

John Moore was interested in the Slate Creek mines and brought his new wife to the ranch at what was then called Rock View in 1902. Their daughter Betty was born three months before John

This road overlooking today's Big Valley Ranch was known as the Goudy Grade and was part of the main route between Winthrop and Mazama until the 1990s, when this section was rerouted. This undated early photograph shows the Goudy homestead in the foreground and the Ventzke homestead in the distance.

was killed in a snow slide near the Chancellor Mine. S. Virginia ran the ranch to make a living for her daughter and herself. When Betty was old enough to attend school, S. Virginia rented out the ranch and moved to Twisp, where she ran the Methow Valley Inn for many years.

Betty Moore married Frank Holec and moved back to the ranch in the 1930s. They continued to live on a portion of the property until at least the mid-1960s. George Cooper built a little sawmill by the pond in the 1940s. Most of the land was owned by the Cooper brothers, Larry and William, until it became part of the Heaths' ranch.

The Albert Ventzke homestead was west of the Moore place in the area where the Big Valley Ranch shops are located. A bachelor, Albert built a log house and cleared most

Brothers Albert and Emil Ventzke at Albert's homestead between Winthrop and Mazama. Emil homesteaded up the Chewuch River. Another brother, Charles, was an engineer with an office and home in Winthrop.

Elinore Kent Drake and her son Gordon stand in front of the old Rock View Hall in 1950.

of the fields. His log house burned down, so he moved into a 14-foot shack across the road.

Around the curve and beyond the shops is a little bench just above the road on the right (north) side. This was the site of the Rock View Hall, a popular early-day gathering spot built as a grange and dance hall. It is said that more dances were held here in the 1920s and 1930s than in any other spot in the valley. Over time the hall fell into disrepair. It was torn down in the 1960s.

About five miles from town, across from the Big Valley corrals, is a house built by Wayne Carrell. Next to that is a house that started as a miner's cabin that was moved to a piece of land the Jim Holcomb family bought from Carrell. The cabin was added onto over the years. The next place down the road was built by Logan Graves. The house burned down in the 1940s, leaving only a shed, which collapsed in the heavy snow winter of 1994-95.

Roy Kumm said that the Cooper boys (George Cooper's sons) were living in the Graves house before the fire and "they would jump out of bed and go to town to eat breakfast and leave the electric blanket on, and that's what set the house afire." This part of the valley got electric power about 1940 but apparently safety practices had not yet been learned.

The H.H. "Hank" Johnson homestead house, later known as the Cooper place, was moved up valley in the 1990s.

The little house that sits on the property today was moved from a half mile up the valley. It had been the old Rock View School that sat above the road near the Cooper place. Joe McCauley owns it today.

The next property up the road to the west, just past mile marker 187, used to have a white house with a screened porch and a barn built by William Wehmeyer, who came to the valley in 1892. The house was restored in 1996, but the barn was destroyed in the winter of 1994-95.

The next house was built by Wehmeyer's son, Charlie. It was occupied by Walt Holcomb for many years. Walt sold the house to Doug Greybeal, who also took over Walt's job when he retired from the Rural Electrification Administration.

The homestead house of H.H. (Hank) Johnson was next to Charlie Wehmeyer's house. Hank was Charlie's uncle. The Cooper family later bought the Johnson homestead and it often is called the "Cooper place" despite its origins. The house was moved up valley to a site below Little Boulder Creek in about 1993.

The family of William Wehmeyer, who came to the Methow Valley in 1892, gathers at a future home site. Note the rock outcrop in the early-day photo and how the vegetation has changed in the 1990s photo below.

The Charles and Lena Boesel homestead dates to 1889, when it was settled by Craig Boesel's great-grandparents. It extended from the hillside to the river. Boesel Canyon and Boesel Creek, both on the homestead, were named after the family. Maps from the turn of the 19th century show a sawmill and school were temporarily located on the Boesel place.

At one point the Boesels sold the homestead, but the purchasers went broke and couldn't make their payments. Charles had died by then, so Lena got the ranch back and asked her son, Albert, known as A.J., to run the ranch, which he did. In later years, A.J.'s son Floyd owned and operated the place until Harold Heath bought it in 1967 and it became part of Big Valley Ranch. Jessie Smith, a Rock View mill worker, built the house down the grade on the left.

The next place, owned by Ernest and Leona Elder, extended on both sides of the road. There were 10 Elder children, all of whom attended the Rock View School. The family was typical of subsistence farmers in the 1920s and 1930s. They cut wood and traded it to the store in Winthrop for things they couldn't raise such as sugar, flour and coffee. They also traded beef, chickens and

The Charlie Wehmeyer homestead house in the 1990s, occupied by the Walt Holcomb family.

Carl Perry's house

turkeys. They gave deer hides to the Indians who regularly camped by the river near Goudy Grade and in return, the Indians would bring them beaded gloves and moccasins made from half the hides for their kids. The Elders' house burned down but the crab apple tree is still growing.

In the mid-1920s Carl Perry built the house and barn on the right about seven miles from Winthrop. The place had been homesteaded by Fred Wehmeyer, who mostly worked for the U.S. Forest Service, but it was Perry who made the most improvements.

At this point in our journey from Winthrop to Mazama, Grizzly Mountain is on the right. A few feet from the present road, east of mile marker 185, one can still see Indian paintings on the rocks. To the left is where the Fender Mill once stood. The old road turned left before the mill and went down to the river, where there was a low-water crossing known as the Perrine Ford. It came out just above Hancox Creek across the Methow River.

Today the Fender Mill site is covered with cottonwood trees and brush. However, when the mill was operating, there was a large pond where the fish screen now sits. The mill, a large burner, shops and several small buildings that housed some of the mill workers were a few hundred feet south. The mill operated mainly during the summer, but all winter teams of horses and men hauled logs. Bill Stewart said "at one time they had twenty six outfits working." Part of the mill burned at one point and was rebuilt.

Mill ownership went from Fender to Cecil Wetzel, who went broke in 1937. The mill was in receivership when Otto Wagner purchased it in 1939. Wagner eventually tore the mill down and moved it to Twisp, where the Wagner Lumber Company became a major valley employer.

The Fender Mill pond was just down river from the Weeman Bridge.

The area across the river from the Fender Mill was known as the McKinney Mountain area. A ford across the river was near the Bert Perrine and Will Morrow places. Hamilton Hancox (sometimes spelled Hancock) had homesteaded this area. Adjoining were the sites on which John McKinney, for whom the mountain was named, built his cabin and Lester Hollaway started his ranch.

This one-lane steel Weeman Bridge stood until 1988, when today's concrete bridge replaced it.

Weeman Bridge to Mazama on the Goat Creek Road

The Weeman Bridge was named after the H.A. Weeman family that homesteaded the land on both sides of the river above the Fender Mill. Over the years, several bridges were located at the site. A bridge built in 1911 or 1912 was washed out by high water in 1932. The next bridge was washed out during the 1948 flood. A one-way steel bridge replaced it and stood until 1988, when the highway was rebuilt and today's two-lane concrete bridge was installed.

The Weeman house and barns were on the hill to the right as you start up Goat Creek Road toward Mazama. The homestead extended down the hill and across the river, where the family grew a big field of red clover because it was too wet to grow alfalfa and other crops.

The Don Drake family lived on the Weeman place from 1962 to 1985. The original house burned and was rebuilt by Clarence Stout.

The Joshua Cassal ranch was farther up Goat Creek Road. Homesteader Burt Perrine sold it to Joshua when Burt took over his father-in-law's place (the Hancox place). The house and barn were on the bench above, just below the field. Joshua irrigated out of Fawn Creek and put up enough hay for 30 or 40 milk cows and two barns.

The original road went up Fawn Creek, came back along the bench, and followed the river. The present road alignment was established in the early 1970s about the time

Prospector Alec McLean holding Wayne Grant on the porch of the Mazama Post Office, which probably was located in the Angus McLeod building in the mid-1920s when this photograph was taken.

the North Cascades Highway opened. Goat Creek Road was rebuilt and resurfaced. The main entrance to the Edelweiss development is located on Goat Creek Road.

Ed and Lucy Walsh, an Indian couple, lived near where the Edelweiss campground and utility building are located today. Ed cut logs and worked in the mill. Teacher Helen Morrow remembered their daughter Hattie as a third grader who could braid her own hair. As part of an assignment to describe a classmate using adjectives, another of Helen's pupils said Hattie "had eyes brown as an unpainted house." In those days paint was an uncommon luxury and most houses were a rich, weathered brown.

The log house and old barn farther along the road sit on land homesteaded by a bachelor named Jake Grazen. Guy Pitt later lived there. He did a little farming and cut logs that he hauled to the mill. But Guy was remembered for the considerable time he spent drinking beer – "about two gallons a day," according to Roy Kumm.

Guy was famous for his home brew during Prohibition. The old-timers who recalled visiting Guy's place said he would haul up bottles from his well, where the beer was kept cool, and everybody would sit under the willow tree enjoying the brew. Guy's nickname was "Two Tone" because when he got excited his voice would crack. Guy's house is gone, as is the log house built there later.

Goat Creek Road enters U.S. Forest Service land at this point and continues past U.S. Forest Service Road 375, which follows Goat Creek, goes down a hill, through a gully and on to the present bridge over Goat Creek. The creek once ran through the gully, but the flood of 1948 changed its course.

Joshua Cassal's original homestead, HES 199, is just past the new Goat Creek bridge. Josh found the land and staked his claim in the winter. When the snow melted he found that all he had was a pile of rocks. Nevertheless, he built a three-story boarding house on the north side of the road with 13 or 14 rooms. The Montana Mine was operating farther up Goat Creek in those days and Josh rented rooms to the miners.

It is also believed that the first Mazama post office opened in 1900 on the first floor of Josh's boarding house and that it was run by Minnie McCain Tingley. Minnie had two daughters by her first husband, Huey Tingley, who apparently deserted the family. Minnie later married Jack Stewart, a mining engineer from Scotland who owned the next place up the road, HES 203.

Jack, who adopted and raised Minnie's daughters, originally had bought the Red Shirt Mine south of Twisp in 1896 and put in a stamp mill. He moved the mill to the American Flag Mine at Mazama in the early 1900s, and later supervised the Bonita Mine. When Jack filed a survey of his claim on Flag Mountain in July 1903, it included the Gwalia, Uncle Sam and Central lodes as well as the American Flag. The map also showed mine buildings including bunk, cook and coal houses and an assay office. Years later, a brush fire burned what remained of the stamp mill.

The Stewarts built a lovely home and barn that became one of the showplaces of Mazama. They raised dairy and beef cattle after Jack quit working the mines. Minnie and Jack retired to California in 1941. Their house stood empty for many years on the property, which by then was owned by Walt and Nella Foster. In the 1970s it was remodeled as a guest ranch for summer and winter visitors. Unfortunately, it was destroyed by a suspicious fire the day before it was to open as the Buckhorn Ranch. No one ever was charged with setting the blaze. Plans to rebuild were made, but the cost of an architect and new construction proved to be too great for the owner.

Jack Stewart's three-story boarding house known as the Way House with Flag Mountain in the background.

Angus McLeod homesteaded HES 113, on the south side of Goat Creek Road, just down river from the present Mazama Community Club. Angus did a little farming, but he also built a hotel, bar and boarding house for miners. The Mazama Post Office also was located in the McLeod building.

The W.H. and R.E. Morrow homestead south of Mazama on the west side of the Methow River. (Date unknown)

McKinney Mountain to Mazama on Highway 20

Crossing the Weeman Bridge and driving to Mazama via Highway 20, the first land to the left is part of the onetime community of McKinney Mountain, which sat across the river from the Fender Mill. Today the McKinney Mountain area is served by Wolf Creek and Kumm roads. The remains of an old log cabin that belonged to Mar Perrine can be seen at the east end of the fields off Wolf Creek Road.

Mar may have been the homesteader, but in 1921 the Morrow family bought the place and built the houses and barns. The house is still there, as are remnants of the barn and outbuildings. The Allison family later owned the place and today the cross-country ski training hill known as "Bob" memorializes Bob Allison, who was an early supporter of the cross-country trail system.

The Hamilton Hancox homestead is next to the Morrow place. It was farmed in later years by Burt Perrine, Hancox son-in-law. The concrete remnants of a potato shed are all that remains of the Perrine place.

Julius Ramm had the next claim of 120 acres, pursuant to a 1910 homestead patent signed by President William H. Taft. The place changed hands several times. The little house and barn built by Dale Allen, are gone although a garage remains.

Ed Allen, Dale's father, cleared the land and built a house on what at that time was called Lucky Jim Road (Wolf Creek Road now). Today the place is owned by contractor Jeff Brown and his wife, Alicia, who operate the Brown's Farm tourist accommodations.

The original Lester Hollaway place was against the hill off Kumm Road. (Ed Allen was Lester Hollaway's brother-in-law.)

John McKinney staked his claim in the 1890s a little to the east, in the middle of the valley at the end of McKinney Mountain Road (now called Kumm Road). The Harry Briggs family later homesteaded the site.

Frank Kumm, Roy's father, bought the place from Briggs in 1924. Frank added to

WEEMAN BRIDGE TO LITTLE BOULDER CREEK

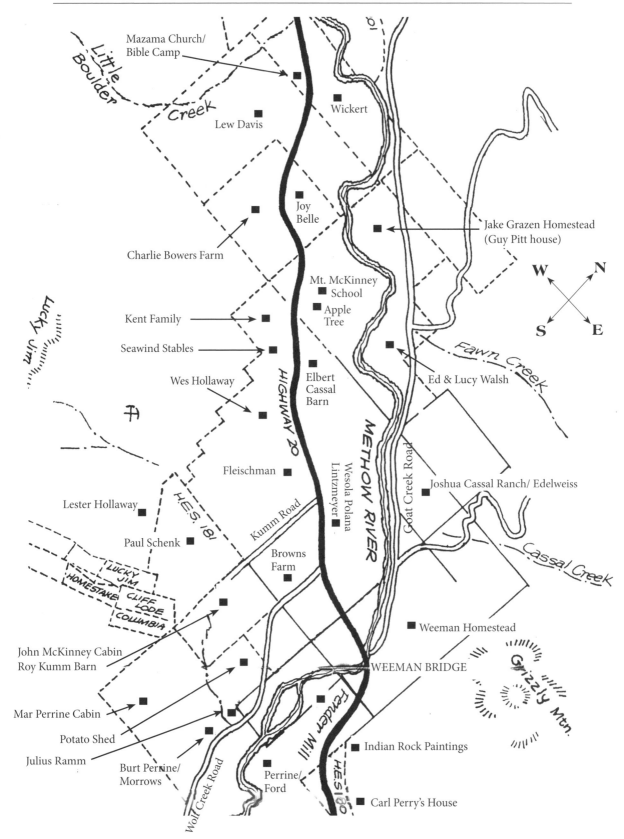

Mazama Church/
Bible Camp

Little Boulder Creek

Wickert

Lew Davis

Joy Belle

Jake Grazen Homestead
(Guy Pitt house)

Charlie Bowers Farm

W   N

Mt. McKinney
School

Apple Tree

S   E

Kent Family

Seawind Stables

Fawn Creek

Lucky Jim

Wes Hollaway

Ed & Lucy Walsh

Elbert Cassal Barn

HIGHWAY 20

METHOW RIVER

Fleischman

Wesola Polana
Lintzmeyer

Joshua Cassal Ranch/ Edelweiss

Lester Hollaway

Goat Creek Road

Cassal Creek

H.E.S. 181

Kumm Road

Paul Schenk

LUCKY JIM
HOMESTAKE
CLIFF
LODE
COLUMBIA

Browns Farm

Weeman Homestead

John McKinney Cabin
Roy Kumm Barn

Grizzly Mtn.

Mar Perrine Cabin

Fender Mill

WEEMAN BRIDGE

Potato Shed

Julius Ramm

Indian Rock Paintings

H.E.S. 130

Burt Perrine/
Morrows

Wolf Creek Road

Perrine/
Ford

Carl Perry's House

The remains of the Lester Hollaway claim in the 1900s. The farmstead grew over the years. The Bernbeck and Campbell families were among its owners.

the house and Roy and Doris moved in after Frank's death. On January 16, 1957, it was 20 degrees below zero and a fierce wind was blowing when a chimney fire started and burned the house to the ground. The Kumms rebuilt that summer and lived in the new house until they moved to Winthrop. The house was remodeled by owners Mike and Cindy Hastings in 1991.

Moving up valley across Kumm Road, Paul Schenk claimed HES 181, which was next to Lester Hollaway, who bought the land, along with HES 182, in the early 1920s. The Hollaways farmed and raised seed potatoes.

The Fleischman place was on the southwest corner of Highway 20 and Kumm Road. The Fleischmans bought it in 1923 from an old bachelor homesteader named Clayton. The house and barn sat back near the mountain next to the willow trees. The house on Highway 20 was built in 1947. Dennis and Lilly Smith have rented it from the Glen Woodward family since 1985. The Woodwards also raise cattle and farm in the Okanogan Valley. During the summer when he has cattle on the range, Verne Woodward lives in a mobile home east of the house. The Woodwards are the last of the cattle ranchers in the Mt. McKinney area, which was devoted mainly to cattle and dairy cows in the old times.

George Lintzmeyer's place was across the road. He built the house and barn that still stand. Shiril Cairns ran a horseback riding and packing operation on the land when it was called the Rock-

The Fleischman family house was built in 1947. Today it is occupied by the Dennis Smith family

The George Lintzmeyer farmstead was called the Rocking Horse Ranch for a number of years. The light-colored wood on the right side of the old barn is part of an addition, one of many changes made by the current owner.

ing Horse Ranch. Prior to that time, the Button family owned the property for some years. They built a snowmobile race track in 1969 in a large field by the road west of the house. They converted an outbuilding to a snack bar and scheduled competitions during the winter. Although the elaborate operation seemed a good way to make use of the Mazama snow, it lasted only a few seasons.

In 2003, the ranch was purchased by Michal Friedrich, a Seattle dentist originally from Poland, who remodeled and restored the Lintzmeyer barn and house, had a new steel house built and put in a soccer field.

The next house up valley on the right is said to have been built by Bob Kifer, but it is not known who cleared the fields or farmed the land. The John Motzkus family lived there for many years and raised hay for horses.

The John Motzkus house.

The remains of an old barn built by Elbert Cassal, one of Joshua's sons, used to lie on the north side of the road. Howard Weller built the original house, which sat by the willow tree that still stands. The house burned down and Elbert put a trailer there in later years. Elbert farmed, mined, logged and at one time tried running a trucking service to Mazama from down valley. His barn was torn down in 1994.

Bill Stewart bought a parcel of land across the road to the south of Wes Hollaway. Bill's house and barn have long since vanished. Wes Hollaway, Lester's brother, purchased the property and subdivided it into 40-acre plats.

Today some of this land is part of Seawind Stables, a horse operation that breeds race horses on the west side of the mountains, then sends the colts to the Methow until they are ready for the track.

The Elbert Cassal barn stood near a great weeping willow tree that was in the yard of the original house, which burned down. The barn collapsed in the 1990s.

Several houses sit on the southwest side of this stretch of road. The first house in the subdivision was said to have been built by Bob Scott. Kenneth Dick occupied the house in the 1950s. It is part of the Seawind property, as is the next farmstead, which includes a house and barn built by Floyd Kent. The Kent family lived there from 1931 until 1943.

The Charlie Bowers family bought a plat from Wes Hollaway and in the 1930s built the two-story house, barn and outbuildings. Craig and Ginni Tissell have refurbished the place, saving the look and feel of the original home. She has a gift shop in one of the outbuildings.

Stan Dick, Kenneth Dick's brother, remodeled the little building just west of the farm, which was moved there from the Mazama Queen Mine, so it became the family home. Stan cleared some of the field behind his house and raised hay. He sold to a developer who built a campground on the property called Liberty Bell Campground. The A-frame house was the campground office. The property later became a residential subdivision.

The Mt. McKinney School sat across the road from the Kents, on the northeast side, near a lone apple tree that is still growing today.

The Charlie Bowers house and outbuildings, including barns, chicken coop and a storage building, that was moved to the site from the Mazama Queen Mine in the 1950s, when the Dick family lived there.

Upriver a few hundred feet, there was a small house with a dirt floor that stood until the 1970s. It was the home of Napolean Bowes, a well-known character in Mazama from the 1940s to the mid-1960s.

Moving west up the valley from the present Liberty Bell subdivision (called the Woodlands today), the next homestead was that of the Youngblood family. Bill Stewart remembered this area as having many very large fir trees that were specially logged for custom milling for the power house at Chelan Falls. The Fender Mill spent weeks on that job.

Robert Sloane had a 160-acre homestead on both sides of today's road. There are two houses on the north side. The first was built by Guy Wyscaver. The white house adjacent to the highway was built by Robert Sloane. Andy Russell later farmed the land for a number of years. The Bible Camp next to Robert's place is on land homesteaded by Lew Davis.

Karl Wickert had the next homestead, which also crossed today's highway and stretched down to the river and across Little Boulder Creek. The house sat on the north side of the road. It burned to the ground in the 1960s and all that remains is a garden of beautiful poppies to brighten the landscape each spring.

The small white building on the south side of the road served as the Mazama Community Church for several years. The building was moved from Little Boulder Creek near what is now the entrance to the Devin ranch. The building had once been the home of the Wickerts' daughter Marie, who married a fellow named Beryl Crawley.

Tom Sloane, Robert's brother, homesteaded the next property, HES 202. Tom was Martha's father and he gave the west 40 acres of property to Martha and her husband, Bill Stewart, who lived there for 50 years. The house, barn and chicken coop were still standing in 1996, but were no longer the showplace they had once been. The buildings were demolished in 2005 when Frank Kline bought the property and built a house and barn in the middle of the field.

The apple tree in full bloom.

The one-room Mt. McKinney School was across the road from the Kent home, next to an apple tree that is still growing.

Napoleon Bowes, right, helps Doug Devin fix a fence in about 1967. Napoleon's hat is made from an alfalfa seed bag rolled up on the sides.

The Mazama Community Church occupied the former Crawley house, which was moved from Little Boulder Creek to where it sits today. A new church was built down valley in 1986.

Tom Sloane owned HES 200 and HES 202, adjoining homesteads. The ownership of HES 202 was in the name of Nancy Sloane, who was Tom's mother and Martha Stewart's grandmother.

HES 200 was held by Tom until Josh Graves bought the place and built the barn. Aaron Burkhart purchased it in 1958. The Burkhart family farmed the entire tract until the 1990s, when they sold some parcels. Aaron Lee Burkhart, the son, still farms part of the place. He raises horses and is a backcountry outfitter and guide.

Two early homesteads border the road adjacent to the present Mazama Road. On the south is HES 81, which was Harley Wehmeyer's place, and on the north was Fred Patterson's place, HES 82. The story goes that Lou Wehmeyer, Harley's brother, filed on HES 82 but failed to "prove up" on the land and Fred Patterson got it, which made Lou and Fred bitter enemies for life. Harley later gave Lou at least 30 acres off the east side of his place, where Lou built the little house and barn that still stands by the road. On the

The Tom Sloane homestead is now owned and farmed by the Aaron Lee Burkhart family, which also operates a riding stable.

The Do Drop Inn of the 1970s.

east end of the Patterson place, a fellow named Jones built a little sawmill by the river that operated for about four years solely by sawing the logs off HES 82. Apparently the Mazama area grew very fine trees.

On the south side of the highway where it joins with Lost River Road is HES 83, which Will Looney homesteaded. Andy Russell had a few acres on the east side of HES 83 on which he raised chickens and a milk cow after he quit farming down valley. He constructed a building from parts of a cofferdam used during a Columbia River hydro-electric construction project. The Russells had a gas pump and café, and Gladys Russell did the cooking. Called the Do Drop Inn, it lasted only a few years.

Karl Duffy, the previous owner of the Devin ranch, mentioned that he didn't think the eating experience was enhanced by Napolean, a frequent visitor to the cafe. Duffy said Napolean "smelled pretty stout" inside a building.

Andy's property also was a collection spot for old iron for many years. He kept busy in his retirement collecting scrap iron and piling it in front of his house. The iron remained until Highway 20 was built in the 1970s.

The Do Drop Inn as it looks today with a facelift.

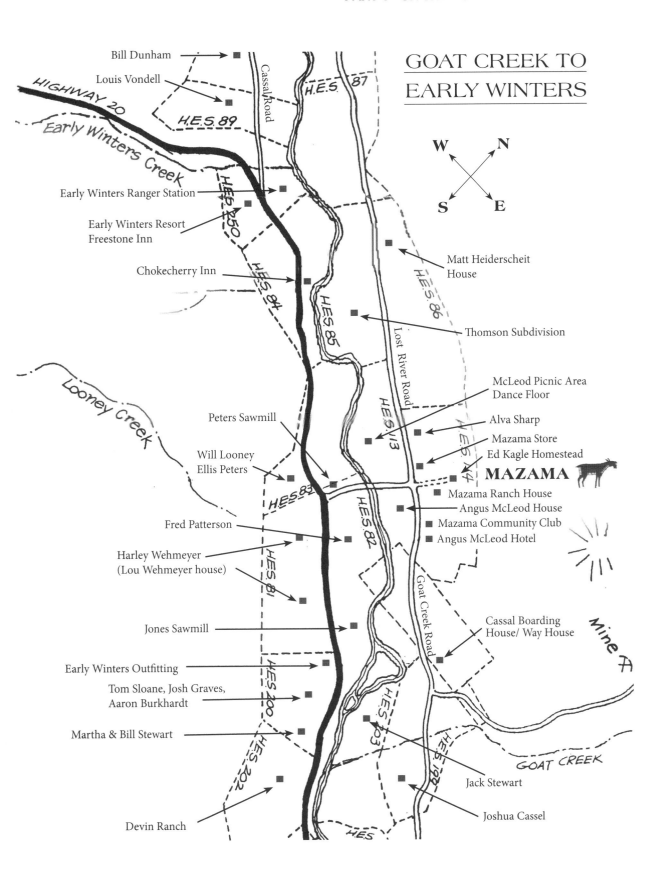

GOAT CREEK TO EARLY WINTERS

Bill Dunham

Louis Vondell

HIGHWAY 20

Early Winters Creek

H.E.S. 89

Cassal Road

H.E.S. 87

W   N
S   E

Early Winters Ranger Station

Early Winters Resort
Freestone Inn

H.E.S 250

Chokecherry Inn

H.E.S. 84

Matt Heiderscheit
House

H.E.S. 86

H.E.S. 85

Lost River Road

Thomson Subdivision

Looney Creek

McLeod Picnic Area
Dance Floor

Peters Sawmill

H.E.S.13

Alva Sharp

Mazama Store
Ed Kagle Homestead

Will Looney
Ellis Peters

H.E.S 14

MAZAMA

H.E.S 83

Mazama Ranch House

Angus McLeod House

Fred Patterson

H.E.S. 82

Mazama Community Club

Angus McLeod Hotel

Harley Wehmeyer
(Lou Wehmeyer house)

H.E.S 81

Goat Creek Road

Cassal Boarding
House/ Way House

Jones Sawmill

Mine A

Early Winters Outfitting

H.E.S 200

Tom Sloane, Josh Graves,
Aaron Burkhardt

H.E.S 103

Martha & Bill Stewart

H.E.S 190

GOAT CREEK

Jack Stewart

H.E.S 202

Joshua Cassel

Devin Ranch

H.E.S

Ellis Peters operated this sawmill in a field near the Mazama cutoff from Highway 20. A fire destroyed the sawmill. The house in the background is part of today's Freestone Inn property.

Mazama to Early Winters on Highway 20

Will Looney came to Mazama about the same time as his brother-in-law, Fred Patterson. They claimed homesteads at the same time. Will got HES 83, next to Copper Mountain (now called Sandy Butte), and Fred took HES 82, by the river.

In later years, Harvey Peters bought HES 83 and he and his son Ellis built a sawmill opposite the barn on the northeast side of what is now Highway 20. The Peters lived in a small cabin by the lower property line and cut timber off their land. They made apple boxes in their shake and planing mills for the Nickell Brothers Packing House.

Ellis Peters married Martha Pollard, who came to Mazama to teach and boarded with the Peters. They bought the sawmill in 1933 and started building their house with lumber from the mill. They finished the house, which stands today at the corner of Highway 20 and Lost River Road, in 1938, the same year the mill burned to the ground.

HES 84, next to the Ellis Peters' place, was homesteaded by Albert Parkinson. Not much is known about Albert, but in later years Bill Fulton farmed the place and built a house and barn near the river. At one time Bill's cabin was the temporary home of the Mazama school. Later, it became the Chokecherry Inn, a bed-and-breakfast owned by Darrell and Marlene Ford until 2004, when it was purchased by Bob and Susan Turner. A broken water pipe caused extensive damage during the winter of 2006-07. Bob Wise, Ellis Peters' son-in-law, built the house on the north side of the highway.

Loys Taylor homesteaded HES 250 on the south side of the highway. It was pur-

Ellis Peters' home in the 1990s.

chased by Les Hollaway, who later sold it to Jack Wilson. Wilson started building the Early Winters Resort in the late 1940s. Three cabins on Early Winters Creek, a barn and corrals were built first. Four more cabins near the Early Winters ditch followed.

The original ford and county bridge crossed Early Winters Creek near the U.S. Forest Service ranger station at the northeast end of the present Early Winters Campground.

Seven homesteads on what became known as Cassal Road were cut out of the wilderness upriver from Early Winters Creek. This particularly beautiful area faces Goat Wall and has views from every angle, but for the pioneers it held exceptional hardships. They were isolated, had marginal soils and coped with three times more snow in winter than fell in nearby areas.

Louis Vondell (also spelled Lewis Von Dell) was the first to stake a claim next to Early Winters Creek, HES 89. Louis was mostly a blacksmith, but he built a classic house. He is best known from the boyhood recollections of his neighbor, Bud Short. Bud recalled that Louis ran a few cows and made his own wine. Wine-making was probably essential, since he was known to consume it in great quantities. Bud remembered seeing Louis spill a glass of wine on the table, then scoop it back into the glass with his dirty hand. The event made a lasting impression on young Bud.

The Louis Vondell homestead near Early Winters Creek.

The Vondell house today. The Vondells sold their place to the Warren Willis family. They sold it to the Len Millers, who farmed a bit and raised Malamute dogs before selling it to the Early Winters resort development partners.

He also remembered that when he was 85 years old Louis got a nail embedded in his foot, which got badly infected. Another neighbor, Harold Grant, had a Model-T Ford and drove Louis to the hospital in Wenatchee to have the foot examined. Bud said Louis "raised hell with the doctors and nurses" and claimed that his foot just needed to be "stomped on," which he tried to do himself by stomping up and down the hospital hallway, which only made the foot worse. The doctors and nurses finally got him on an operating table to amputate the foot. However, he died on the table. Louis was buried in Sullivan Cemetery in Winthrop in 1925.

Mazama pioneer Charlie Woods, on the right, puts up hay in the 1930s with the help of three unidentified friends. Bill Voight probably built this barn.

Goat Wall School students posing here are, back row from left, Dwight Corrier, teacher Mildred McDermott, Alice Peters, Kenneth Corrier, Earl Short and Bud Mays; front row from left, Carl Peters, Clara Corrier and Bud Short.

After Louis died, Warren Willis took over HES 89 and farmed the land. He remained there until the 1960s, when he sold the tract to the Len Miller family.

Bill Dunham had the next place, HES 90. The exact location of the house is not known. Both HES 89 and 90 stretched from Driveway Butte to the Methow River.

Alva Welch claimed HES 91 and built a house and barn. The barn is gone. The remains of the house are still standing, but it was moved down the road a mile or so. The house is sometimes called the "rattlesnake house" because a group of local children on horseback once saw a rattlesnake slink under the house. They talked about the house as the rattlesnake house a number of times and the name caught on. Rattlesnakes are frequently seen in the area.

About 1910, William (Bill) Voight was homesteading HES 92. He was a carpenter, but like most men in Mazama he also worked in the mines. He built a nice house and barn on the tract. At the time, the house was the only painted house in the valley – pink and white.

The Short family bought the house in 1922. Ranson Short worked for the Great Northern Railroad and lived and worked in Wenatchee before buying HES 92. His family of three boys and two girls ran the farm. The oldest girl, Edith, married Harold Grant and they moved into the vacant house next door on HES 93.

The youngest Short child, Bud, was born the year after the Shorts moved onto HES 92. He lived there until he left for World War II in 1942. He remembers going down the lane of trees at the end of the field to the "Black Bear Ford," which crossed the river by Goat Wall Creek.

The school was located for a short time on the opposite side of the Methow River. The children would cross the river on a big, old, fallen cottonwood tree. After a one-room school was built on HES 94 to serve children in the Early Winters area, they no longer had to walk the log. Members of the Short family lived on HES 92 and HES 93 for many years.

By the time Don and Dorothy Shafer bought the place in the early 1940s, the "painted" house had been moved up valley a few hundred yards

The Dennis Overturf homestead house where Earle and Selma (Sloane) Short later lived.

from its original site. The Shafers eventually owned HES 91, 92 and 93. They enlarged the fields and obtained a range permit. They ran more than 300 head of cattle. The remains of an assortment of farm buildings are on the land today.

HES 93 was originally homesteaded by Dennis Overturf. He built part of the little house that lies in ruins at the upper end of what is still called Shafer Field or Shafer Meadows. Dennis had some cows, and his wife cooked at the boarding house in Mazama. Dennis was only 40 years old when he died in 1929. His son was just a baby, and his wife and children lost the homestead because they couldn't pay the taxes. That's when the Shorts, and later the Shafers, took on the farm.

The Calloway Cassal homestead.

Calloway Cassal, another of Joshua's sons, claimed HES 94 and later purchased HES 198, which adjoined it on the upriver side. Calloway built the house and barns, most of which are still standing. The large barn on the same level as the road was built using trusses that Calloway salvaged and hauled across the river from Archie Green's defunct sawmill on HES197. The big barn was used for the Methow Music Festival at one time.

HES 198 had been homesteaded by John and Temperance Arnold, who built a house on the bank overlooking the river at the very upper end of the present-day field. Their house burned and the family moved. John died in 1914 at the age of 57 and Temperance Arnold eventually lost the place to the bank.

Calloway Cassal, an industrious fellow, later acquired HES197, which extended across the river toward Mazama. His entire field was enclosed by a deer fence to protect his hay crop. The story is told that Calloway had so much trouble with deer that he shot large numbers of them. He would stack the carcasses, then call the Washington Department of Fish and Game to pick them up. After repeated occurrences and the payment of damages to Calloway, the department decided it would be prudent to build a fence around the field, which was fine with the owner. A contract to build the fence was put out to bid and Calloway himself was the low bidder. Everyone was happy – Calloway had a good paying job building his own fence, the game department no longer had to pay damages or pick up carcasses and the deer no longer had to worry about being shot.

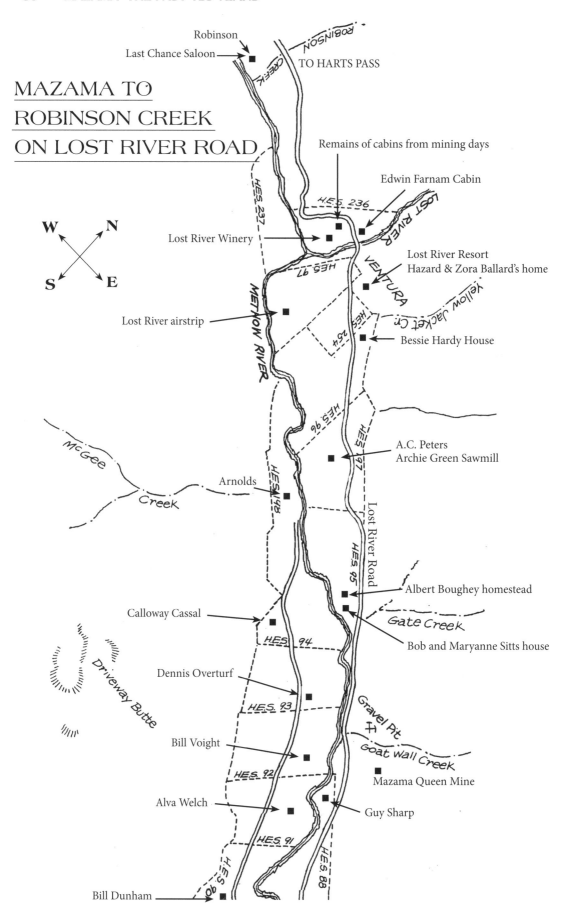

MAZAMA TO ROBINSON CREEK ON LOST RIVER ROAD

Robinson

Last Chance Saloon

TO HARTS PASS

ROBINSON

CREEK

HES 237

HES 236

Remains of cabins from mining days

Edwin Farnam Cabin

LOST RIVER

W N

S E

Lost River Winery

HES 97

VENTURA

Lost River Resort
Hazard & Zora Ballard's home

Yellow Jacket Crk

Lost River airstrip

METHOW RIVER

HES 254

Bessie Hardy House

HES 96

HES 97

A.C. Peters
Archie Green Sawmill

McGee

Arnolds

HES 98

Creek

Lost River Road

HES 95

Albert Boughey homestead

Gate Creek

Calloway Cassal

HES 94

Bob and Maryanne Sitts house

Driveway Butte

Dennis Overturf

HES 93

Gravel Pit

Goat Wall Creek

Bill Voight

HES 92

Mazama Queen Mine

Alva Welch

Guy Sharp

HES 91

HES 88

HES 90

Bill Dunham

The Ed Kagle homestead.

Mazama to Robinson on Lost River Road

What today is called Lost River Road used to be called Slate Creek Road. It was the route the miners took to the Slate Creek Mining District. Most of today's commercial activity in Mazama is on HES 114, the homestead of Ed Kagle (spelled Kagel in some references). His land was on the right side of Lost River Road, north and south of today's main intersection in Mazama, including where the Mazama Country Inn and Mazama Ranch House are located.

Ed probably came to Mazama as a prospector because his name is on a number of early claims in the area. In 1914 he recorded the Mazama Queen Mine on Goat Wall. He had a five-stamp mill operating from 1931 to 1938.

Ed apparently sold some pieces of property for commercial use; for example, a store and post office adjacent to today's community building. He also donated land for the school and grounds and is known to have sold at least one parcel for a home site. Occasionally he got land back for lack of payments.

Considerable timber was taken off the homestead. Ed grew strawberries and hay, some of which he sold, and he made moonshine. His house was up against Goat Wall on a road that today would pass in front of the Mazama Ranch House. He died in 1940.

Allan and Bob Stookey owned the ranch at one time and built a house that today is part of the Mazama Ranch House. The Stookeys sold the place to Charles and Martha Bowers and their sons Donald and Harold in 1948. The Bowers had a herd of 60 Herefords and raised 250 Leghorn chickens. They built the barn and moved the cook house from the Mazama Queen Mine to their land and converted it to their chicken house. They sold the place in 1959 to the Wally Eggleston family. They farmed it until the 1970s, when they sold it to Cal Merriman and a group of investors who subdivided most of it and built the Mazama Country Inn.

In 1995, Steve and Kristin Devin, the author's son and daughter-in-law, bought the barn that Charles Bowers had built and other buildings and land from Cal and turned them into today's Mazama Ranch House, which has accommodations for tourists and their horses.

The Stookey house, which is now the Mazama Ranch House

Bill and Vi Pederson built the Mazama Store and Post Office in the 1940s on a portion of HES 114. Bill paid Harold Bowers, Charlie's son, $90 for one acre of land.

The post office previously was near what is now the southwest corner of the junction of Goat Creek and Lost River roads. Wilfred "Wink" Byram and his wife Gretchen bought the store and post office from a Mrs. Braun in 1939 and sold it in 1944 to Allan and Bob Stookey, the brothers who owned the ranch across the road. Wink says it was hard to get supplies to stock the shelves during World War II, plus he had an offer to work for the Wagner Lumber Company, which he took. He ended up spending most of his working life as a logger.

Allan Stookey

The Pedersons, who lived in a mobile home, had the post office inside their store. Bill kept adding onto the buildings as business grew. Several owners later, Jeff Sandine purchased the business and buildings in the 1990s. Jeff demolished all the old buildings and built a large new store and post office. However, the mail service was short lived. Jeff could not abide the red tape and bureaucracy that went along with running a post office and moved it out of the store after only a few months. Today, Mazama has its own zip code and some residents have a post office box next to the community club. But most residents are on a rural mail route out of the Winthrop post office.

Angus McLeod's homestead was across the road from HES 114, closer to the river. Matt Heiderscheit was Angus's neighbor and he claimed HES 85. Matt later

Grady Schmidt Stookey

Matt Heiderscheit built his own house, shown here in 1995, and helped build many others in the valley.

Guy Sharp was one of several Sharp family members to build homes in Mazama. Last Chance Peak is in the background.

bought HES 86 from Jeremiah Bader, so his property stretched from Goat Wall to the Methow River.

Matt, a bachelor, built himself a large, three-story house near Goat Wall plus a barn and outbuildings. He was a fine old German builder who worked as a carpenter and also kept a herd of about 30 milk cows.

In later years, A.L. Thompson bought HES 85 on the river side of the road and subdivided the property into more than 30 long, narrow tracts.

Continuing on toward Lost River, there is a cliff on the right side of the road. HES 87 is on the left, or river side. Henry Countryman held the original claim on this land, and later it belonged to Jim Lewis. Jim built a barn, had a few cows and "irrigated the rocks" to get some pasture. Bill Stewart remembered that there were a few spots where Jim got "some pretty good hay." Careless hunters caused the place to burn down in the 1950s.

HES 88 was located next to the river and was the home and claim of Guy Sharp. Guy cleared the place and farmed various crops, but what everyone remembers are Guy's big fields of cabbages. Guy sold cabbages and homemade sauerkraut. He also created an early subdivision of sorts, Sharp Acres, a row of small tracts along the road. Larry Higbee built small houses on some of the tracts. At that time the area was called Prenticeville. Guy's house still stands by the big rock at the bottom of Goat Wall.

At this point, the road runs at the base of Goat Wall for some distance. Just before Goat Wall Creek is the site of the Mazama Queen Mine, which was worked off and on over many years. The operation consisted of a mine high up on Goat Wall and a mill a few hundred feet off the road that used water from Goat Wall Creek. The mill hired as many as 40 to 50 men at times.

The next property, HES 95, starts at Gate Creek and lies to the left of the road. It was claimed by Albert Boughey, who built a cabin and worked away at the land enough to prove up his claim. Albert was best known in the community as a violin player. He sold to H.C. (Harvey) Peters, who built a small sawmill on the property. Peters previously had owned a mill down valley next to the Mt. McKinney school.

Bessie Hardy and her attractions may be gone but her once fine house still stands on Lost River Road.

The next owner of HES 95 was Charlie Woods, who was known for his gardens. Charlie grew wonderful vegetables because the warmth of Goat Wall prevented frost long after the rest of the valley's gardeners had lost their gardens for the season. In 1984, Bob and Maryanne Sitts built a large log house and barn on the property and, assisted by the wall, continued to raise a big garden.

Harvey Peters also homesteaded the adjacent HES 197, which he later sold to Archie Green. Archie took over Harvey's sawmill business and built a new mill on the property. The mill eventually was taken out by a landslide and Archie sold the property to Calloway Cassal.

HES 96 is the next place down the road. It appears that the land between HES 95 and HES 96 went unclaimed for a period of time. William Robinson homesteaded HES 96 and kept the land for many years. It is thought that William was not related to the Robinson brothers who had the original camp on Robinson Creek, which is named for them. A small 60-acre homestead claim was taken out of the middle of the property in later years.

On the right side of the road, before the road to Yellow Jacket Creek, is a house with a stone foundation built by Bessie Hardy and Alva Sharp, her companion and for a time her husband.

Bessie, known locally as "Lost River Bessie," ran a roadhouse that served chicken dinners. She was said to have sold Alva's moonshine and her own home-brew along with her favors to the menfolk who passed by on their way to the mines. Bessie was popular locally. She occasionally would be jailed for some infraction, such as delivering a car full of moonshine to the Rock View Hall. Inevitably, a neighbor would show up the next morning and bail Bessie out of jail. In later years Bessie ran a roadhouse between Winthrop and Twisp where she rented rooms, served chicken dinners and had girls working upstairs.

Just up river from Yellow Jacket Creek is an area known as Ventura, which was a large tent city at the time Col. Thomas Hart, onetime manager of the Eureka Mine, was having the road that bears his name built to reach his mining interests. However, he left the

Bessie Hardy in 1921.

Bessie Hardy and Ed Kagle

area before the road was complete. Speculation that a town would develop at Ventura obviously was quite premature.

HES 97 borders Lost River where it meets the Methow River and was claimed by Harry Mayfield, who later sold it to Hazard Ballard. Harry had been active in the early days of the Slate Creek mines and at one time held the contract to carry the mail to the mining camp at Barron. Hazard had a pack string of 40 animals and ran a hotel at Robinson in the early 1900s.

Up the Methow River beyond the Lost River Bridge is HES 237, claimed by Charles Mayes and later sold to Zora Ballard, Hazard's wife, after she was widowed. The Ballards are the namesake of today's Ballard Campground, which is on Forest Service land.

By the 1980s, part of HES 97 had become the Lost River airstrip and the site of a large subdivision of vacation home lots developed by Pete Arnold, a World War II veteran and colonel in the Air Force. There are hundreds of lots in the subdivision. Pete's vision was that weekenders would fly in to use them. Hazard Ballard's house used to be located at the upper end of the property where the road turns to go down to the river. In the 1960s, a restaurant known for its chicken

Hazard and Zora Ballard's home at Lost River.

dinners was located across the road toward the Methow River.

The remains of a number of log buildings lie across the Lost River Bridge. These are said to be the remains of a supply station for the mines and a base for the dog teams that were used to transport supplies and mail during the winter.

On the right side of the road after crossing Lost River is HES 236, a small homestead

These remains of log buildings in the Lost River area are said to be left from the days when dogsleds were used to service the Azurite Mine in winter.

claimed by Edwin Farnam, who built the log cabin adjacent to the road in the 1920s. The homestead extended across the road to the Methow River, including the site of today's Lost River Winery.

The road continues on to Robinson Creek, the site of Robinson where in 1900 a post office and the Last Chance Saloon were located. This facility served a sizeable population of prospectors and men working on the Harts Pass road. For a short time Guy Waring operated one of his Methow Trading Company stores at Robinson to serve miners heading to the Slate Creek mines. Why this land wasn't homesteaded is not known.

In the 1930s, a large Civilian Conservation Corps camp was located at Robinson Creek and remained there for several years. By the 1990s there was no visible trace of the settlement. However, if one scrapes the dirt, an occasional piece of metal or a nail turns up, testifying to the existence of early enterprise.

This cabin at the confluence of Robinson Creek and the Methow River was being used as a store and post office when this photograph was taken in July 1900.

PART II

A Chronological Account of Development in the Mazama Area

1st Lt. George Benjamin Backus Jr., explored the upper Methow Valley in 1883.

1st Lt. George Washington Goethals was second in command of the 1883 expedition and wrote the report submitted to the U.S. Army.

Chapter 1
Early Records of Exploration

Early exploration of the Methow Valley by whites is recorded partly in the journals of U.S. Army officers who traveled with scouting parties searching for routes across the North Cascade mountains for military and economic purposes.

First Lieutenant George Benjamin Backus, Jr., who came to the Northwest with Gen. William Tecumseh Sherman in 1883, led such a scouting party. Sherman, known for his scorched-earth campaigns against the South during the Civil War and his post-war subjugation of the Plains Indians, was General Commander of the U.S. Army from 1869-1883. As part of a visit to western military outposts the year before he retired, he also toured the Okanogan country and camped near Lake Osoyoos.

The following account of the Backus scouting party is taken mostly from an article in the June 1983 issue of the journal *Northwest Discovery* edited by Harry M. Majors.

Backus, a native of Pennsylvania and a graduate of the U.S. Military Academy at West Point, was in his early 30s. He arrived at Lake Osoyoos with Sherman's party on Aug. 12, 1883, and was promptly ordered into the Methow country to find a rumored pass (probably Harts Pass). Protecting the northern frontier, locating potential railroad routes, facilitating settlement and spurring economic growth were among the federal government's objectives at the time.

Miners claimed to know a way across the mountains north of Cascade Pass, according to an 1882 report by Lt. Henry H. Pierce. Backus also had been with the earlier Pierce scouting party, so he knew approximately where the pass would be found if it really existed.

First Lieutenant George Washington Goethals, 25 years old at the time, was ordered to accompany Backus to make maps and record the events of the trip. Goethals later became a professor of engineering at West Point and was appointed by President Theodore Roosevelt as chief engineer and first American governor of the Panama Canal. (He replaced chief engineer John Frank Stevens, who was credited with "discovering" Stevens Pass in 1890.)

The Backus party of 1883 consisted of six men, six saddle animals, four pack mules and one hound dog. They left Lake Osoyoos the morning of August 15 and proceeded along the Similkameen River.

The land they entered had been Indian country reserved for Chief Moses and the Columbia River Indians under executive orders issued in 1879 and 1880. The borders of what was popularly known as the Moses Reserve were roughly the Canadian Border, the Cascade Crest, Lake Chelan and the Okanogan, Stehekin and Columbia rivers.

However, an executive order issued by President Chester A. Arthur in February 1883 – just months prior to the Backus journey – and another issued by President Grover Cleveland on May 1, 1886, opened the reservation, including the Methow Valley, to non-Indian settlement and mining.

Backus would have been familiar with the following journal entry made by a member of the Pierce party in 1882:

"At the foot of the ascent (of War Creek, up the Twisp River valley), I came with my Indian guide (Swa-u-lum) upon an old miner and his younger comrade cooking their noon-day meal of mountain-goat's meat. They begged me to spare them a little flour, of which they were nearly destitute, in exchange for a shoulder of mountain goat. The request was granted much to their relief, when the train was unpacked that evening, and thenceforth they clung to us for companionship to the very top of the Cascade range where bewilderment, uncertainty of the locality and the loss of their strongest pack-horse down the rocks turned them homewards a dejected and disappointed pair."

The older of the two miners probably was A.M. McGee, (spelled McKee in some references) who claimed to have lived in the mountains for 32 years, the last seven in the Methow searching for golden quartz. He appeared to be well informed on the country and the Indians.

McGee told the Pierce party that the Methow River valley was unoccupied by whites and that he regarded it as the finest he had seen east of the Cascade Mountains for stock and grain. In an article published in Snohomish, Washington, in 1877, he is quoted as saying:

"...this river (the Methow) ascends to the summit (Harts Pass) from the south east, by an easy grade, the elevation at the summit is much less than by the Snoqualmie route, and if the decent (sic) to the north west is as gradual as on the east, it would form the best pass in the Cascade range for a wagon or railroad."

McGee said he *"went to the summit, nearly, in the month of January last (1877) and found no snow except on the north hill side."* He was almost certain that this pass was unknown to whites. It was his report of a pass north of Cascade Pass that prompted the U.S. Army Department of the Columbia to conduct further exploration.

McGee was not the only white man who had been in the Methow. Capt. George Mc-Clellan led a U.S. Army expedition to the Methow Valley and Lake Chelan in 1853. That party was searching for a railroad route across the Cascade mountains. However, they went only about half way up the Methow River.

In the spring of 1880, Dick Miller and a party from Spokane came up the valley headed for the mines at Ruby Creek. They camped at Early Winters, waiting for high water to go down.

The Backus party came close to meeting prospector McGee on the upper Twisp River in late August of 1883. At the foot of Lincoln Butte the explorers passed a recently made, deserted camp. Finding a horseshoe and scattered pieces of clothing, they knew it was a white man's camp. Upon returning to Twisp they learned from Indians that two white men had gone along the trail before them. From their descriptions, Backus recognized the pair as the two miners who had accompanied the Pierce party the previous year.

When the Backus party returned from its exploration of the Twisp River, Goethals made the following entry in his journal on September 1, 1883: *"Two days' march from the forks, over the old trail, brought us to the Methow at the mouth of the Twotsp (the Twisp), where camp was made and a delay of two days made, partly for the benefit of our animals, partly to negotiate for the hire of a pony. Corpl. Rheinhardt had walked for the past four days, and his horse seemed to be getting worse. We succeeded in getting a pony and left the Corp'l's horse to the cure of a 'medicine man' until our return."*

On September 4, Goethals wrote: *"From our camp here we followed the Methow on the right bank in a general N.W. direction for two days, making in all 20 1/4 miles. An Indian whom we met near the end of our first day's journey, warned us against proceeding too far on that trail, as marshes would be found (about three miles beyond the mouth of Wolf Creek) to stop our progress, and a return would be necessary, that portion of the trail was used by Indians only for hunting purposes."*

Camp for the night of September 4 was two or three miles northwest of the mouth of Wolf Creek, *"on a small stream whose course is parallel to the main stream, and which sinks a few hundred yards below where we were located."*

The party continued to ascend along the southwest side of the Methow in a northwest direction. On September 5, Goethals wrote: *"We crossed the creek on which our camp was located, and ascended a small hill 175' then following a small valley for about three miles, we came again to the Methow, going along that the rest of the day, by a well marked (Indian) trail."*

Goethal's map shows that his party crossed Little Boulder Creek and made camp about one mile beyond Little Boulder and about two miles below the mouth of Early Winters Creek in what is today the community of Mazama.

His journal entry of September 6, 1883, reads: *"About three miles beyond Camp 18 (Mazama) we crossed a large tributary (Early Winters Creek)...we determined to turn westward and follow this branch to its head. The (Methow) Indians call this the 'Papoose Methow.' "*

Camp on September 6 was on the north side of Early Winters Creek, immediately above the confluence of Cedar Creek. The men explored the area. The journal entry of September 9, 1883, describes pushing forward about three miles and camping just below the confluence of Papoose Methow and probably Silver Star or Cutthroat creeks. A heavy rain set in *"which lasted all night and until late the following afternoon, and which forced us to remain in camp. Our only shelter was a fly of a wall tent that Mr. Chapman had brought for his own use for when we left the main party at Osoyoos we could get nothing in the way of a tent."*

Toward evening on September 10, the storm passed and the air was once again clear. Goethals wrote that he and his men were *"thankful as we had been passing through smoke ever since we left the head of the north fork of the Twotsp. We could see ahead of us the snow covered zigzag peaks resembling those at the fork of the Twotsp, and which did not appear a great distance off, we decided to camp another day, for plenty of good grazing could be had..."*

Goethals noted earlier that they had been traveling in smoke from forest fires almost from the day the trip started and that often their view of the land was shrouded. His reports from the Early Winters area also mentioned good grazing, beaver dams, deer and ample wood and water.

On September 11, Goethals was ill and stayed in camp while the rest of the party started for the summit without a pack train. They were gone all day. Although Goethals' map depicts a small portion of Early Winters Creek above the confluence of Cutthroat Creek, Backus at this juncture chose to ascend Cutthroat Creek instead of Early Winters, probably because he was seeking a route and pass westward to the Skagit.

Cutthroat Creek led him to the southwest, whereas upper Early Winters Creek headed due south. As a consequence, Backus entered a cul-de-sac and missed the opportunity to discover Washington Pass, where the North Cascades Highway now crosses. Backus' misjudgement is understandable because the east side of Washington Pass is so well hidden that one must ascend to the absolute head of Early Winters Creek before the pass becomes visible.

On September 12, 1883, he made his final entry about the Early Winters area, noting numerous signs of deer and bear, among other things. He concluded: *"For those who are now desirous of going up that stream it would be well for them to follow our route as shown by the blazed trees, but they should not follow it with the attempt of getting across the Cascade Range. For hunting purposes the country is certainly a good one."*

Chapter 2

The 1890s
Mining Interests Flourish

Guy Waring's Methow Trading Co. at the gold rush town of Barron on the west side of Harts Pass.

The first recorded discoveries of gold in the upper Methow were in the 1870s by a prospector named C.P. Rowley. They were on Slate Creek with entry from British Columbia along a route so hazardous and expensive that it did not get much traffic. Miners also had been prospecting up Ruby Creek, a tributary of the Skagit River, since the 1870s and eventually they reached Slate Creek. But it wasn't until about 1891 that a mini-gold rush started after prospectors had good fortune traveling from the south over an old Indian trail that went to Slate Creek through what was known as McGee Pass, then Slate Pass and finally Harts Pass.

A.M. McGee was the first white man to learn about and use the route the local Indians described to him. To reach Slate Creek from the west was grueling. Some found it downright hair-raising. The miners found the eastern approach through the Methow Valley easier than the western route.

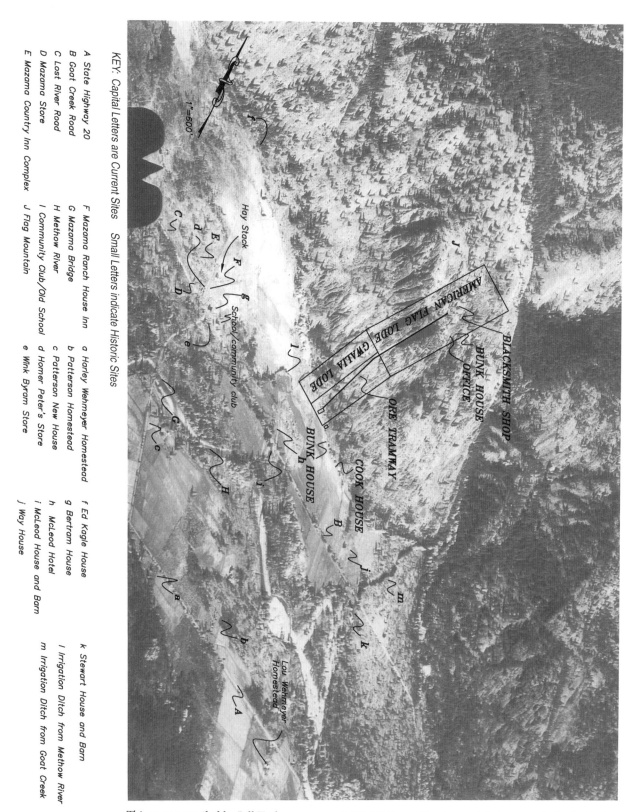

KEY: Capital Letters are Current Sites   Small Letters indicate Historic Sites

A State Highway 20
B Goat Creek Road
C Lost River Road
D Mazama Store
E Mazama Country Inn Complex

F Mazama Ranch House Inn
G Mazama Bridge
H Methow River
I Community Club/Old School
J Flag Mountain

a Harley Wehmeyer Homestead
b Patterson Homestead
c Patterson New House
d Homer Peter's Store
e Wink Byram Store

f Ed Kagle House
g Bertram House
h McLeod Hotel
i McLeod House and Barn
j Way House

k Stewart House and Barn
l Irrigation Ditch from Methow River
m Irrigation Ditch from Goat Creek

This map compiled by Bill Tackman, uses a 1939 US Forest Service aerial photograph for the background. Homestead sites, mining interests and other landmarks are noted.

Winthrop circa 1896.

It was Alex Barron's discovery of the Eureka lode in 1893 that really started a local gold rush. The camp and town that developed were, appropriately, called Barron.

In March, 1895, Col. W. Thomas Hart came into the Methow with financial resources at his disposal and took options on mines at Squaw Creek, in the lower Methow Valley, and in the Slate Creek mining district. Hart was described as "corpulent and courtly." Despite his title, there was no evidence that the Georgia-born mining man and promoter had ever been associated with the Confederate army. And there is no record of his name in a listing of officers. However, bestowing military titles upon oneself apparently was a fairly common practice after the Civil War, regardless of military service.

Hart managed or "experted" the Eureka Mine, which had been prospected a few years earlier. The mine became a big producer. Tons of equipment and supplies to support the mine were carried by pack animals up through Mazama and Robinson on crude trails.

Hart engaged Charles H. Ballard to survey a road along the north side of the upper Methow River, crossing the summit of what was then known as Slate Pass but was soon to be renamed Harts Pass. By mid-April of 1895, Hart had 65 men working out of a camp at Ventura, which was about a half mile down river from Lost River. They were constructing a road from Lost River that climbed past Deadhorse Point, a precarious trail around a rock face with an ugly drop. It was said that an entire string of pack horses, and the packer who somehow survived, plummeted 1,000 feet almost straight down, giving the point its name.

During the first week of June, after only two months of road construction, Hart abruptly paid off his men and departed for Arizona. He had been fired by his syndicate, according to an article in the *Leavenworth Times*, the newspaper published in Leavenworth, Washington, which went on to say, "Extravagant and unnecessary use of money (caused) Col. Hart's tumble from the pinnacle of prominence and power."

It is unclear how far the road was built under Hart. At its narrowest, it was 26 inches wide, requiring wagons to be cut down and horses to be hitched in tandem to navigate it. Apparently two of the Ballard brothers, Charles and Hazard, widened the road to 36 inches and completed it to the summit and down into Slate Creek.

In the 1890s nearly everyone in Mazama was a miner. There were 20 placer claims in Mazama between 1894 and 1899. Many were filed by persons of historic note for reasons other than mining, such as Guy Waring, Col. W. Thomas Hart and Dick McLean.

First Push for a Highway

Between 1893 and 1895, the Washington Territorial Legislature, pressured by mining interests, appropriated $30,000 and established a commission to recommend a route for a highway from Puget Sound to Marcus (an early mining and railroad center north of Kettle Falls) in Eastern Washington.

A reconnaissance party was sent up the Skagit River to Slate Creek and Harts Pass. From there, the party traversed down Trout and Rattlesnake creeks to the Methow River. At least two other routes were considered – from the Skagit River via Thunder Creek, and from the Skagit River over Rainy Pass. The third choice was lower with an easier grade, but was the longest and would have required expensive rock excavation in the Skagit River gorge.

The study was started on July 22, 1893, and in just 50 days, the commission completed its work and adopted the report. Ultimately, the commission decided that the shortest, most feasible route was from the Twisp River over Twisp Pass, down Bridge Creek, up the Stehekin (at the head of Lake Chelan) and over Cascade Pass near Marblemount. The report recommending the Cascade Pass route called for a road width of 40 feet and ordered work to start in the spring of 1896. Obviously, governmental decision-making was much more expeditious in the 1890s than it is today!

Work on the mountain part of the road was done by day labor under the highway commission's supervision. The laborers were paid a daily wage of $2. The foreman received $2.50. Board and room at the five camps was 75 cents per day. Because funds were limited, work was done without a survey except at a few critical points. In areas of heavy excavation, only a four-foot width was graded. Brush and timber were cleared to a width of 16 feet, and rocks and stumps were cleared from the roadway to allow wagons to pass. Bridges were built where needed. Crews completed the entire road, except for clearing a small amount of brush along Bridge Creek, before heavy snow forced them to leave.

The commission was very proud of what it had accomplished in 1896, especially from a national defense viewpoint. It reported that the wagon road provided "a continuous highway for the movement of troops in case of necessity and particularly in protection of the northern frontier." In testimony on what had been achieved, the commission reported that George Rouse, a local miner, rode horseback from the mouth of the Twisp River to the summit of Cascade Pass in one day and a few hours of the next, a distance of 53 miles. This was more than twice as fast as earlier travel time.

The next year, the Legislature appropriated $21,000 for further improvement and an additional six miles of roadway. However, when the crews could get back into the high mountains they found that spring runoff had undone much of their previous year's work. Slides and floods had washed out bridges and sluiced away long sections of the narrow grade. Repairs took the entire appropriation. New construction had to wait. The road was completed in 1899. The commission called it "a good road for mountain country" over which "four ordinary horses can pull 30 hundredweight (of freight) with ease."

However, six years later, Joseph Snow, the state's first highway commissioner, described the road as "a horse trail from Marblemount to the summit of the Methow Range and about 12 miles of wagon trail down the Twisp River."

Local miners didn't benefit from efforts to construct a highway. Travel to the boom town of Barron and mines in the Slate Creek district continued to be up the Methow River past Robinson, around the narrow ledge and wooden platform hung on the side of Deadhorse Point, and over Harts Pass. This route was open to men and supplies all year. Snowshoes and dog teams were used in winter and horses and mules the rest of the year.

Prominent Citizens of the Upper Valley

Guy Waring

During the late 1890s mining boom when Hart was building the road to Slate Creek, there were 1,200 people in the Robinson and Lost River areas and about 2,500 miners in Barron.

When Guy Waring, the Harvard-educated founder of Winthrop and the Methow Trading Company, arrived in the Methow Valley in the spring of 1891, there already were a few settlers in the area – some at Rock View, about seven miles above Winthrop, and some downstream at Sullivan's Flat. Hazard Ballard, brother of mining engineer Charles Ballard, was settled at Lost River.

Waring established squatter's rights on September 29, 1891, at the confluence of the Methow and Chewuch rivers. He and his family spent their first fall in a tent. Cold weather already was settling in, and the family not only cooked their meals on a stove, but also ate them from the stove to keep the food from freezing while they were eating it. In the old western tradition, neighbors soon arrived to help the Warings build their first house.

The following year "the Governor," as Waring was called by his step-children, opened a store, which was the beginning of the Methow Trading Company. The Warings had hauled with them enough supplies and merchandise to stock a small store. Prices were notoriously high, but the early settlers were happy to have the convenience of a store in the upper valley. Waring also served as postmaster.

The winter of 1892-93 was extremely hard, with deep snow and bitter cold. And on March 1, 1893, a fire destroyed the Waring home, store and post office. A 12-by-14-foot root cellar was all that survived of the Waring place. It served as the only store and post office in Winthrop. The Warings spent several weeks in a 16-by-20-foot cabin across the river waiting for the roads to open. As soon as travel was possible, Waring and his family moved east seeking financial backing. Walter Frisbee and later Earl Johnson operated the business while Waring spent the next three years raising money before returning to Winthrop in November 1897.

While the Warings were away many changes had taken place in Winthrop. A bridge was built in late winter of 1894 over the Methow River at its confluence with the North Fork, as the Chewuch River was known to early white settlers. The proud community had barely started using the new bridge when it was washed away in the terrible flood of 1894, which wreaked havoc up and down the Methow and wiped out the town of Silver below Twisp. Hart rebuilt the bridge in 1895 on his march to the Slate Creek mines. By 1896, Winthrop had a blacksmith shop, drug store, hotel and schoolhouse.

The Warings returned with enough financial backing to rebuild. The Methow Trading Company was incorporated in 1897 and it eventually expanded to include outlets in Winthrop, Twisp, Robinson and Barron. A large room on the second floor of the main store in Winthrop gave the growing community a place to meet and hold social functions. It was the scene of many festive affairs.

The Ballard Brothers

Ten years after establishing the first store in Winthrop, Waring patented the townsite and became its first real-estate developer. By then, Charles and Hazard Ballard, two of the four Ballard brothers to live part of their lives here, were among the area's prominent citizens.

About 1895, Charles Ballard, who had come to the Okanogan a decade earlier, located the Mammoth Mine in the Barron area, which he managed for a number of years. A few years later, Charles and Hazard Ballard and Dick McLean filed claims that established the Azurite Mine, one of the valley's most prominent. Charles was active in the mine until his death in 1934. His widow Anna took over their interests in the operation and was involved with the Azurite Gold Company until her death in 1960.

During his life, Charles had been many things, including a civil and mining engineer. Before coming to the Methow Valley, he had laid out the towns of Chelan, Conconully, Oroville and others. He filed the original plat for Chelan in 1889, when Okanogan County went from "the British line" to the Wenatchee River. Charles Ballard also served as probate judge because he was one of the few well-educated men in the county.

Jack Stewart

In the late 1880s, a lode of gold was discovered between Benson and Beaver creeks that would lead to the establishment of the nearby Red Shirt Mine. A few years later, Jack Stewart, a mining engineer from Scotland, came to the valley and purchased the mine. He built a small reduction plant, installed a 20-stamp mill and put a crew of men to work. All went smoothly for a few years. However, Stewart suddenly dropped the mine and moved to Goat Creek near Mazama after he and his company made a deal for the Flag prospect.

Mahlon McCain had discovered a lode of free gold in an 80-foot ore shoot three feet wide. It was about 100 feet above a previous mine at his American Flag Mine on

Flag Mountain. It was this discovery that prompted Stewart to move his stamp mill to Mazama.

Stewart put in a tramway from the mine down to a small reduction plant and set up a flume from Goat Creek for power. Things worked well for several years until one day disaster struck. A loaded tram car near the mine broke loose. It raced down the track, and with its tremendous momentum, drove right through the plant, killing two men working in the mill, including Frank McCain, one of Mahlon's brothers. The runaway car's speed was so great that it curled the track behind the car as it came down. The mine was closed for a number of years. Stewart moved his mining equipment to Slate Creek. After a few years, he settled down to farm. He became one of the first citizens of Mazama.

An article in an 1896 issue of the *Chelan Leader*, then the closest newspaper to the Methow Valley, reported the following:

"This valley is just booming ahead. There have been several large barns put up, 80 x 40 and 60 x 80 feet on the ground, and as high as 21 feet to plates. There have also been several dwellings put up. Mr. McCain, the mining man and merchant of Goat Creek put up a two story dwelling, 20 x 30 feet, with a 16-foot lean-to the whole length. Mr. Frisbee, of Winthrop, put up a neat little cottage.

"Messrs. Frisbee and Hulett have burnt a brick kiln of A-1 brick, almost equal to pressed brick. They also burnt a lime kiln, and in the near future many buildings will be ornamented with auburn craniums.

"The valley is supplied with all kinds of vegetables and some fruit, as several farmers raised from 25 to 100 bushels of apples, pears, plums, peaches and cherries, and nearly everybody raised some small fruit. Hen fruit seems to be the scarcest and is worth 20 cents a dozen. Grain is about one dollar per bushel. Dressed hogs are worth about 8 cents a pound and beef 4 cents. Nearly everybody seems to be living well and to be happy."

By the late 1890s, most miners in the Methow Valley had been drained away by the Klondike Gold Rush of 1897-98. However, at the turn of the century, there were still at least 300 active mines stretched from the lower Methow Valley to the high mountains beyond Mazama. Settlers were beginning to put down roots in the upper valley between Winthrop and Slate Creek – for example, the Ventzkes about five miles west of Winthrop, and the Wehmeyers and Johnsons at Rock View. Well-known pioneer families already had settled into the valley below Winthrop.

By the 1900s, the placer mining claims were about depleted and miners were doing hard rock mining. Mazama literally was circled with claims in various stages of development. Nearly every homesteader had his name on at least one claim.

John McKinney

Although he wasn't a miner, the diary of early settler John McKinney, a Civil War veteran from Phillips County, Kansas, gives insight into what life was like at the time. After the war McKinney was searching for work in the town of Demersville, Kansas. There wasn't any work, and he had been sitting around for almost a week. On Monday, January 8, 1892, he made the following entry: "... being no stock to work with nor will not be for 2 or 3 weeks, I conclude to go to Washington and hunt up a homestead."

McKinney spent the next 10 days traveling around getting ready. On Thursday, January 18, he wrote: "8:30 a.m., jump freight train for Spokane. Fare $2 to ride 125 miles. Ride all night."

On February 3, 1892, McKinney took the stage to Wenatchee and started his search for a homestead. His diary describes the first of a number of walking journeys that would be considered marathons today but were quite routine at the turn of the century. He walked 16 miles up the Wenatchee River, found snow a foot deep, so walked 10 miles down river and spent the night. The next day he walked back to Wenatchee and crossed the river on the ferry. The following day he walked all the way to Waterville (about 20 miles by road today), where he met with some chums to compare notes on land they had seen. He then walked to Badger Mountain (about 10-15 miles) to look at a claim, which he didn't like.

During the next two days, McKinney walked 24 miles up the Okanogan River and stayed with a Mr. Malott. Over the next six days, he worked his way up the Methow.

The remains of a John McKinney cabin, near the source of Hancock Spring. This was probably his second cabin, judging from the description in his diary. Briggs and Kumm families later occupied the land.

One night he put up at Mason Thurlow's home, another at a Mr. Sullivan's house, and yet another at the Ventzke brothers' place, all the while looking for a claim he liked.

On March 23, his diary contains this entry: "Go 3 miles up the river to Mr. Hancock's. Snow too deep to hunt land in timber." This was the spot where McKinney eventually settled, but for the time being, he returned to the Ventzke brother's place and recorded that he moved onto Wolfe's ranch and operated out of there or sat around camp.

Finally, on April 1, McKinney's diary has this entry: "Together with Mr. Hancock, Mr. Williams and T. Wolfe, we pace off my claim, lying west of Mr. Hancock's." (Probably at the same spot Lt. Backus had stopped to water his horse nine years earlier.) The claim had level land, ponds, beaver dams and lots of timber.

Immediately after staking his claim, McKinney went to work laying foundation stones and cutting poles for his log cabin. On Sunday, he started his cabin and "cleaned out the spring and fixed it up with stone, then cut brush at the head of pond." Hard though it is to believe his timing, the diary records that on Monday he started a road and within three days had cut a good wagon road 300 yards to his pond, finished his cabin and roof, put in a door and window, built a bunk and filled it with spruce and balsam feathers (sic) and planted a garden with potatoes, carrots, turnips, rutabagas and sunflowers.

On the third day, the diary contains two short entries that surely were satisfying to John McKinney: "Move into my cabin. Go to bed in my own home."

The morning after McKinney first slept in his own cabin, his diary says he started out at 7 a.m. for the town of Ruby to look for work. It was a two-day walk and he arrived at 4:30 p.m. on Friday. There was no work to be had. His diary records that he wandered to "Loomiston" (Loomis), Conconully and Palmer Lake and sat around camp for the next 10 days.

In the Methow, McKinney, a leatherworker as well as a general handyman, went into the shoe repair business. But an entry made on a Sunday says: "Still looking for work. Get box and fit up a shoe bench with milk cans for pegs and nails and commence sorting them out as they got mixed en route."

On May 1, McKinney finally found a two-week job building a boarding house for a stamp mill. On May 15, he returned to the Methow Valley to resume work on his own place. He got back on a Friday, in time to help his neighbor, Hancock, put up his kitchen.

McKinney was not a young man when he came into this country and the hard life, and maybe the miles of walking took their toll. About 10 years after arriving in the Methow, in 1902 or 1903, McKinney decided he needed care. He was on his way to an old soldier's home on the coast when he was found dead near the train depot in Wenatchee.

The spring and little creek that flow into the Methow River from McKinney's place are now called Hancock Spring. But the mountain that rises above his place is named for him and the whole adjacent area is called the McKinney Mountain area.

McKinney probably never had the actual title to his land, but he was well respected in the community and certainly was considered a homesteader.

THE OWL SALOON

CHAS. GRAVES, Proprietor.

Wines, Liquors and Cigars.

Winthrop, Wash.

The Hotel Winthrop	The Robinson Hotel
H. H. GREENE, Proprietor.	RICHARDSON & KERN, Prop'rs.
	ALL KINDS REFRESHMENTS AT BAR

This Owl Saloon advertisement was published in the Methow Valley News on Jan. 1, 1904. The hotel was run by Guy Waring's stepson, Harry Greene. Hazard Ballard later owned the Robinson Hotel.

Stores at —

PATEROS – TWISP – WINTHROP – BARRON, WASH.

M. T. Co.'s Sawmill

AT ROCKVIEW

Rough Lumber now ready

Planed Stock, Lap Siding and Shingles will soon be a regular product

A 1903 advertisement for lumber sold by the Methow Trading Co., which had a sawmill a few miles out of Winthrop at the time.

Chapter 3

The 1900s and 1910s
A More Diverse Economy Develops

With more settlers arriving, the Methow Valley was no longer just a stopping place for miners bound for the Slate Creek mines. Although prospectors continued to search for gold and some commercial mines continued to operate, the boom days were over. (The Methow Trading Company store in Barron closed in 1905.) Today there still are claims being worked and some gold and other minerals are extracted, but mining, like panning for gold, is mostly a part-time hobby. By the turn of the 20th century the local economy was diversifying, the postal service was expanding and there was a newspaper in Twisp.

The establishment of the *Methow Valley News* in 1902 brought wider communication of social events and allowed for commercial advertising. For example, the January 1, 1904, issue contained an ad for The Owl Saloon in Winthrop, which touted the establishment's wines, liquors and cigars, and carried ads for The Hotel Winthrop and The Robinson Hotel.

On October 28, 1900, Guy Waring had an application prepared for a Robinson Post Office. It was to be located nine-and-a-half miles northwest of Mazama and 13 miles southeast of Barron on Star Route 71382. It was to begin operation between Winthrop and Barron on November 15, 1900. The population to be served by the Robinson Post Office was listed as 10 in the winter and 50 in the summer. The office was to be at a lumber camp and was the last stop before going over Harts Pass.

On June 1, 1900, just a few months before the Robinson Post Office was established, Minnie McCain Tingley established the Mazama Post Office. What is today called Mazama was originally called Goat Creek, referring to the creek that flowed southward around Goat Peak. For some unknown reason, the Postal Service would not accept the name Goat Creek or Goat Mountain. So at the suggestion of Guy Waring, the town was named Mazama. He explained that Mazama was the Greek word for mountain goat. Actually, the word was a Spanish word for a genus of South American deer, but Greek for mountain goat apparently was close enough.

After Minnie, who had two daughters by her first husband, married Jack Stewart, the mail came to their red, three-story house on HES 203, twice a week – by horse and hack in summer and horse and sleigh in winter. Minnie would tie each patron's mail into bundles so that when someone came in on snowshoes, he would be able to deliver to others along the way. She always had a bowl of hot soup to serve the mail carriers before they started their return trips.

After a few years, Minnie found it necessary to give up the post office so she could take care of her mother. She successfully recommended Angus McLeod as the new postmaster. Angus lived a half mile up valley from Minnie on HES 113, where he kept an inn. He ran the post office for the next 15 years.

As described in preceding accounts, many of the original homesteaders and home builders in the Mazama area were miners. F.F. Ventzke was a civil engineer involved in mining. So were his brothers, Albert and Emil. Hazard Ballard came to make his fortune mining in the Slate Creek area and became rich more than once on the mines. However, he was poor between his rich spells and also worked as a packer.

The Rockview Sawmill was on the Methow River on the J.J. Johnson homestead, known in later years as the Cooper place.

Logging was an important part of the local economy. In about 1909 neighbors in the Mazama area began work on the Early Winters ditch to carry water down valley to ir-rigate the fields as they were cleared and converted to crops.

By 1910, named communities were emerging in the upper valley. Robinson and Lost River were at the head of the valley west of Mazama. McKinney Mountain was on the southwest side of the river. Rock View (also spelled Rockview), on the northeast side of the river, was home to an active sawmill. As settlers continued to arrive, more and more land was cleared and houses built. Lumbering became a major industry. The Methow Trading Company sold lumber from the mill at Rock View.

In February 1910, R.E. Johnson and Hazard Ballard bought machinery from a saw-mill in Chelan and moved it to Rock View. For about 18 months their partnership oper-ated as Johnson & Ballard. Hazard later bought out his partner (who was to become his father-in-law). Business was good and by September 1912, Hazard was planning to get larger machinery for the mill.

The week of September 12 the newspaper reported that "For the past week about 25 teams a day have been hauling lumber from the mill, but on hand are hundreds of thousands of feet in the yard."

Rockview mill workers about 1912. Left to right: Bill Jones, Joe Ebbet, Roma Johnson holding his daughter Genevieve, Dennis Overturf, Will Thurlow, Harvey Lyons and Lou Wehmeyer.

Winthrop's Newspaper

In August of 1912, William Brinkerhoff, who had purchased the defunct *Winthrop Eagle* newspaper, began publishing the *Methow Valley Journal* in Winthrop. The paper (the name of which changed for awhile to *Met-how Valley Journal* and then back to Methow) greatly aided communication in the upper valley. It carried notices and announcements about the activities in busy Rock View. For example, there was notice of a special election to select the site for a new school, an announcement about the Rock View Grange's Monday meetings and news of a dance scheduled for December 15 with music by the Sanstrom Orchestra.

The *Journal* also reported on practice games between the Winthrop and Rock View basketball teams. One game ended in a 17-15 victory for Winthrop. (Basketball was played during the winter while the Rock View mill was closed.)

When spring came in 1913, the contract was let to build the new school at Rock View. The contracts also were let for Winthrop's grand new two-story brick school house, which was to cost $13,000. The lumber was to come from Hazard Ballard's Rock View Saw Mill.

By June 1913, Ballard had driven more than a million feet of logs down the river to his mill. The run started when the river was up from the spring melt, but a spell of cool

A Hazard Ballard log drive on the upper Methow River about 1915. He once owned the Rockview mill.

weather caused the river level to fall again and handling the huge old-growth logs was very difficult in low water. To the mill workers' credit, only one serious jam occurred. It was loosened with two cases of dynamite and only about 2,000 feet of logs were lost.

On the social side, the *Journal* reported that the Fourth of July in Winthrop was "a gala day long to be remembered..." Early in the morning people began to assemble for the interesting program. At 10:30 the Winthrop band appeared on the street and marched to Riverside Park. Rev. Berg started with a speech then the band played again before dinner.

"A number of tables were provided and the feast was spread featuring yellow-legged chicken. In the PM the crowd was called together by the band for races. First of these was the nail-driving contest for ladies, then the muddle race. After this the crowd proceeded to the ball park for the finest exhibition of ball playing ever seen on the grounds. The married men took on the bachelors and defeated them 5 to 3. After the game there were the following contests: sack race, egg race, balance pole, ring riding. Then followed the Grand

The Met-how Valley Journal started in Winthrop in 1912. This Aug. 7, 1913, edition included stories about the importance of the creamery to the upper valley and a man chased by a bear as well as a list of all out-of-valley people who checked into the Forks Hotel.

Ball by the band and the fireworks were numerous. Music for the dance was furnished by the Stokes orchestra which went till 12 o'clock."

The *Methow Valley News* of June 14, 1912, reported that "settlers up the West Fork of the Methow are building a wagon bridge across Early Winters Creek. This will be a great convenience as there is a long period each year that this stream cannot be forded."

Harvey and Lula Peters

Harvey Peters arrived in the upper valley in 1912 with his wife Lula and their seven children. He filed a claim on an abandoned homestead above Gate Creek, HES 197, where Bob and Maryanne Sitts' large log home and barn sit today.

Harvey came from Kentucky and West Virginia, where his father and brothers were timber men. He married Lula Hale in 1899. He heard about the tall trees in the Western states, and based on this "hearsay" he packed up his family and mill hands, loaded a freight car and headed for Bellingham, Washington. He started a mill and sold it. He also tried farming for a few years. But by April 1912, Harvey, Lula and their seven children were homesteading five miles above Mazama.

They built a house, cleared four acres and planted feed to winter cows and horses. Harvey worked out of the valley during harvest in the Big Bend wheat fields to buy flour, sugar, coffee and staples for winter. Lula delivered babies as far down valley as the Weeman Bridge.

Ellis Peters, one of their sons, once found a stash of old 60-gallon lard cans filled with dishes, bedding and other personal effects on the property. Up on the hill behind the place there was a mine digging and a log cabin with a rifle leaning against the wall, but no evidence that anything had been disturbed. Ellis never knew who the homesteader was, or what happened to him, although he speculated that he might have been attacked by a bear or cougar.

The Peters were a musical family. Harvey played the fiddle, guitar and old pump-type organ. Lula played harmonica, and the children all could sing and play some instrument. They played for dances in the schoolhouse and parties.

One night, after a dance at the Rock View Hall, the Peters family was bundled up on their sled gliding home over the snow. From behind them out of the dark they heard a whipping and hollering and shortly a man pulled up and yelled, "Say, did you get all your kids? We found this one sleeping under a bench." Sure enough, it was young brother Jay.

At one point the Peters clan sold the mill to Archie Green and left the valley for their Kentucky homeland, but they returned in 1925 and re-started the shingle mill. There was little money, so shingles were traded for almost everything. The family sold the mill and moved closer to Mazama on the southwest side of the river. Harvey set up another mill where he cut lumber and wood for apple boxes. That's the mill he later sold to his son Ellis and daughter-in-law Martha Peters.

Ellis turned to farming after the sawmill burned in 1938. He died in 1993. Having lived in Mazama for more than 60 years, he was one of the few to witness its change from an Indian hunting ground to a recreational playground. In his life, Mazama went from being the very end of the road to being the beginning of the North Cascades cross-state highway.

Many members of the Winthrop Brass Band were from the upper valley and many played a role in the development of Mazama. First row, left to right: W.E. Singer, Mose Brinkerhoff, Ferd Haase and Charlie Walters. Second row, left to right: Si Walter, Edgar Allison, Ferd Haase Sr., Reuben Hotchkiss, Carl Boesel and Alva Sharp. Top row: Amos Stokes, Andy Hall, Bill Haase, Roma Johnson and Al Haase.

Jack and Minnie Stewart

After Jack Stewart married Minnie the postmistress, he adopted her two daughters, and set to work improving his homestead, HES 203, a little less than a mile east of Mazama. The house built, he turned to putting up a barn that attracted considerable attention. It was circular with a large silo in the center and took more than 100,000 feet of lumber to construct. While such barns were common in New England, they were unknown here.

The barn was described as having a walkway down the middle and stanchions for 30 milk cows facing out under the hay storage area. "The barn was about 60 feet long and 40 feet wide and 36 feet high at the peak with a hay carriage track two feet below the peak," according to the recollections of Vernon LaMotte. The barn was destroyed by fire in the 1960s.

Jack had a large cattle and dairy operation for many years, but he always spent a couple of weeks prospecting at his mines every summer. When the Stewarts retired in 1941, they moved to California, where they spent their last years.

While logging and building were the focus of much attention in the valley, mining continued to be a factor in the local economy. In early 1914, the *Methow Valley Journal* reported that:

* "W.V. Looney and Dennis Overturf take the contract to do assessment work at the mines on Goat Creek."

* "The contract to carry the mail to Slate Creek and Barron has been let to Harry Mayfield."

* "The Montana Mining Co., who (sic) has several good claims on Goat Creek, unloaded a carload of mining machinery Wed. & Thu. Wm. Voight and Wm. Looney superintended the unloading in Pateros."

* "A narrow gauge wagon road is being built up Goat Creek to haul a small stamp mill to test ore at the mines there."

In November 1915, the new community hall at Rock View finally was finished and a large crowd attended its dedication, marked with a performance by students and faculty from the Mt. McKinney and Mazama schools, according to the newspaper.

"Professor Dow opened the program with a fitting address complimenting the public spirit of the community in constructing the magnificent building. A sumptuous supper, games, and a get together meeting comprised the evening's entertainment."

The next week, a large crowd assembled again, this time for a basket social and dance. Some $22 from the sale of baskets went toward paying for the hall.

The Montana Mine up Goat Creek closed for the winter the week of November 10, 1915. It was a good time to close because that winter got off to a dramatic start in Mazama. By the first of December, there was three feet of snow on the level. Will Looney's new barn collapsed from the weight.

But the spring of 1916 came early. Water appeared in the river the first week of March. This was good news because it meant that some of the wells that had gone dry in the winter would be replenished. To prepare for high water, a suspension bridge was put in at Mazama and a cable bridge with a cage was put across the Methow below the Weeman Bridge.

By May, spring activities were in full swing. The Mazama baseball team had a dance and "cafeteria supper" at the Rock View Hall to raise money. Baseball practice was held on the local diamond – east of the current Mazama Bridge. The May 4, 1916, issue of the *Journal* reported that "The first auto of the season reached Mazama with Reuben Hotchkiss at the helm."

Jack Stewart built this barn, typical of New England barns, but unique in the Methow. It burned in the 1960s.

World War I

When World War I came, young men in the Methow registered for conscription draft into the United States forces. In June 1917, a Home Guard regiment was formed for North Central Washington, headquartered in Wenatchee. The goal was to register 1,000 men. The registrations for the Methow precinct were as follows: Mazama 11, Winthrop 76, Twisp 73 and Carlton 15. The Methow had its own battalion. Non-commissioned officers would meet one night per week in addition to conducting regular drill on Tuesday nights.

In July of 1917, it was announced that Okanogan County would be required to furnish 143 men and 42 would come from the Methow. By lottery, Mazama residents Dennis Overturf and William F. Voigt were chosen, but they were not among those to be sent off the following month.

Years later a monument was erected at the Okanogan County Courthouse honoring Okanogan County men who died in World War I. Two names from the Methow Valley were included: Joe Biart and Captain Hughie Fraser, both of Winthrop.

By World War I, telephones were in use throughout the valley, except in Mazama, and in some areas up to 22 families would be on the same line. Telephone operators used a special ring combination during the war to signal that everybody should pick up the receiver and listen to big news about the war.

This log house, built by homesteader Lou Arnold, served as an early Mazama school. This is probably the class of 1917 or 1918. From left, Arnold Parkinson, Keith Patterson, Ray Patterson, Ella Wehmeyer, Nadine Hollaway, Carol Patterson, teacher Opel Peters and Hazel Patterson, Carol's twin.

The year 1917 also brought changes to educational facilities in the area. Lou Arnold's log cabin on HES 84, just west of the Mazama Bridge, became a one-room schoolhouse after he moved to new quarters. Before that time, the school was located on the other side of the river near the McLeod Hotel. The move to the Arnold cabin lasted only a few

This cable bridge, near the present Weeman Bridge, served the Mt. McKinney area.

years. A new, permanent school was built on the north side of the river in 1921 and it was used for many years. That "new" school building is today's Mazama Community Club, the red building that sits just south of the main intersection.

End of An Era

On August 3, 1917, the *Methow Valley News* published a small news item that in many ways marked the end of an era in local history: "Mr. and Mrs. Guy Waring were passengers out yesterday for the Atlantic coast where they will remain indefinitely. Rbt. Greene succeeds to the management of the business at Winthrop."

Although sometimes controversial, there is no question that Guy Waring was a most influential pioneer in the Methow Valley and all of Okanogan County. He was involved in nearly every aspect of the community and its economy. He had been a cattleman, merchant, orchardist and public official. He owned everything from a saloon to a saw-mill. And his enthusiasm affected the growth and attitude of the whole community. His departure was definitely newsworthy.

The Hollaways and Looneys

About the time John McKinney was leaving for the old soldiers' home, growth in the Mazama area was brisk. Homestead claims were being filed, timber cut, farm fields planted, houses built and dreams turned into reality. The dreams of the Hollaways and the Looneys, who moved from Spokane to the Methow Valley, would have a significant impact on the community of Mazama. The following account is taken in large part from Ethel Hollaway's memoirs.

Lester Hollaway, the son of a Nebraska homesteader, and Ethel Callahan, the daughter of a Minnesota school teacher and a mining enthusiast, met in Spokane. Ethel's father, Sylvester "Ves" Callahan, had taken the family, including Ethel, her brother, and her sister Olive, on a trip during the summer of 1904. They went up to Canada, down to Oroville and up the Methow across Early Winters Creek.

The Lester Hollaway homestead in the Mt. McKinney area.

Ves Callahan heard about a mine on Copper Mountain (now called Sandy Butte) in Mazama. He had always been interested in mines. So five years later, after his daughter Ethel had married Lester Hollaway and his daughter Olive had married Will Looney, Ves made both sons-in-law a deal: he would give each of them $150 to go to the Methow and work for the summer on a prospect mine located on Copper Mountain. Lester and Will bought a team and a hack and, with their wives, packed up equipment from their homes. The two couples headed for Mazama with the idea of spending a summer in the beautiful Methow Valley.

It was June 1909 when they reached the swollen Columbia River at Brewster and found that the cable ferry wasn't working. The boat coming upriver could catch onto the cable but would lose it near the top of the crossing. Finally, after waiting three days, the boat made a trip upriver and managed to hold the cable.

The Hollaways and Looneys were the first wagon on the ferry and they had a frightening trip across the roaring, muddy Columbia. But by noon they were among trees on a mountain road traveled by freighters up into the Methow Valley. They stopped the first night at Gamble Mill and the second night at Joe Lydas' place. They then went down Benson Creek into the Methow Valley and on to the town of Twisp.

The party proceeded up the south side of the Methow past the Thompson place, over

Wolf Creek, and up a rough, steep hill into heavy timber country. Whoever was driving at the time wasn't paying attention and the wagon ran into a tree. The collision broke the wagon tongue, so the party camped on the spot until they made a new tongue. The next day, they drove on and reached Copper Mountain, where they found the spot Ves Callahan had described.

Lester and Will were struck by the beauty of the surroundings – tall mountains, beautiful yellow-trunk pines and an impressive bluff called Goat Wall. They were in thick pine, grass above their knees, and so jubilant in their surroundings that they hopped off the hack and rolled in the lush grass. They turned the horses loose and the first thing the horses did was treat themselves to a good roll in the grass, too.

The next morning, Lester and Will packed the horses, went up the mountain along the creek and easily found the mine. Since it was near the creek on a level place, it was a good camping spot and they stayed there while they did their promised assessment work. By the time they finished, both the Hollaway and Looney families had made up their minds to locate in the valley instead of returning to Spokane. Lester filed on a piece of land at the foot of McKinney Mountain.

There was an old house and good well on Lester and Ethel's land and a sign in the yard that read: "Meals – 25 cents – 35 cents for a gouge."

Will bought a relinquishment (homestead land that had not been improved) from Roma and Pauline Johnson at the foot of Copper Mountain, where a creek (later named Looney Creek) emptied. He found a cabin by the creek and moved in his family.

The Marvin Perrines lived next to the Hollaways in a little log cabin at the foot of Lucky Jim Mine. Marvin was working the mine and gave Lester a month or so of work. It was a tough job. It was so cold that when the men came down for dinner, icicles were hanging off their clothes. They would strip, put on dry clothes, and after eating, return to face the tunnel and water coming from the rocks at every angle. The workers took an old sewing machine and other items for pay, and somehow managed to survive the winter.

Ethel Hollaway took this photograph of the first Mazama bridge, which was approximately where today's bridge is located.

Will Looney's sister Minnie heard about the beauty of Mazama and became excited about pioneer life. She married Fred Patterson, in Cheney, Washington, and they decided to join the Looneys. They filed a claim on HES 82 on the river next to the Looneys. Fred cleaned up the land and started farming. The farm remained in the family for several generations. Greydon Patterson, Fred and Minnie's son, lived there. And the late Larry Patterson, Fred's grandson and owner of Cascade Concrete, kept a few cows on the place into the 1990s.

Transportation was quite a challenge for early settlers in the Methow Valley. The roads were a problem. The river was an obstacle. When the water was low, the Methow River could be crossed at the Perrine Ford, about a mile down river from the present Weeman Bridge, and the well-traveled road to town could be used.

Later, there were two ways to cross the river to get mail and visit. One was a narrow cable bridge across the river at Mazama. Olive Looney got used to walking this shaky bridge and had fun shaking it to scare her friends.

The second way to cross the river was by a cage-and-cable bridge near the Perrine Ford, across from the McKinney Mountain area. To cross, a person would step into a little cage and then pull themselves across on the cable.

In about 1913, the Weeman Bridge (named for the family that lived adjacent to it) was built. The Hollaways and the Weemans became close friends and Lester Hollaway was put in charge of building the approach to the bridge. It was Lester's first job that paid real money.

Lester was involved in other activities that benefited the entire community. For example, homesteaders had made a small irrigation ditch that served a bit of the McKinney Mountain area, but it wasn't satisfactory. So Lester got together with the Morrows, who lived just below him, and built a larger ditch system. They went about a mile and a half above the Weeman Bridge and got all the homesteaders who lived in between to help with construction. They surveyed the entire ditch with a level and straight edge.

Despite Lester's activities, the Hollaways were far from financially secure. They needed to raise more money if they were going to do more than merely exist. Their parents had helped them out a little from time to time, but this was not a long-term solution. So Ethel Hollaway decided to teach at the Mt. McKinney School. She earned $75 a month, which enabled Lester to hire some help.

During the winter, Lester would ride a horse through the snow, dragging a log to make a trail to the schoolhouse for Ethel and the students. He would make a short cut through the woods and across the field. Ethel would ride her horse to school, "but turn her back towards home." (A trained horse would return home if directed.)

The second year Ethel taught, Lester was able to buy five little Jersey heifers. This was the start of their dairy herd. Considering Ethel was a city girl from Spokane, she adapted well to the role of farmer's wife. At one point she hand-milked 10 cows while Lester milked 16. However, her milking career came to an abrupt end when a notorious kicker stepped very close behind her. She asked Lester to move the cow away. He assured her the cow wouldn't kick and told her to stand up and move out. Well, she stood up, and sure enough, the cow kicked her. Ethel set down her pail and said to Lester, "I hope you enjoy milking my ten cows along with your sixteen." She never milked again.

One of the things Ethel liked about living in the McKinney Mountain area was the small number of snakes on that side of the river. She had seen a bull snake but never a rattlesnake. On the other side of the river where her friends the Weeman's lived, rattlesnakes were numerous. The farmers killed many rattlesnakes and cemented their dens so they couldn't get out. During one snake roundup, 135 rattlers were killed as they came out of a den.

Ethel, along with the rest of the community, was thrilled by the arrival of telephones and electricity in 1915. "What a joy that was," Ethel recalls. Of course, the phone was a party line and all the settlers joined in visiting with one another. "I remember Mrs. Wehmeyer and Mrs. Carrol always said good night (over the party line) before they went to bed." To have telephones, and lights in their houses and barns, brought great benefits and joy to Mazama residents. The arrival of each was a major event.

Lester and Ethel Hollaway with their daughter, Nadine, about 1912.

Ethel was in a good position to compare locations in the Mazama area because Lester bought and sold many pieces of land over the early years and the couple moved fairly frequently. He bought a timber claim across the road from their McKinney Mountain home, along with HES 250 – the place at Early Winters that was later owned by Jack and Elsie Wilson. The Freestone Inn and Early Winters cabins are on that property today.

Lester and Ethel owned the Gunn Ranch, high above today's Big Valley Ranch, for a number of years, and the old Wehmeyer home in Rock View, old man Brigg's place above them and a piece of land next to the Weeman place. They paid for improvements to their properties with profits from their resales and from the sale of logs to the Rock View, Fender and Gamble sawmills.

Lester was forced to sell one of their ranches after he became very ill and underwent an operation in Pateros. The family left the valley for awhile, but returned later along with Lester's father, whom they cared for until he died. They lived in Winthrop until Lester had to take the ranch back.

It was not an easy time. Lester returned to ranch life while Ethel stayed in town and boarded teachers. Lester's brother Wesley came to the valley with his family and lived on the ranch with Lester. (Eventually, Lester acquired the Frank Lang place, just above his own place, for Wesley and his family.) Wesley moved out when Ethel moved back to the ranch for the summer. Lester bought a herd of angora goats that ate most of the brush off a new field. Then a Mr. Coffin came from Twisp to shoot out the stumps. Lester sold the goats and it wasn't long before he had yet another field of alfalfa.

In 1936, Lester rented his fields to the Northern Seed Company. The arrangement did not work because the fields apparently were not good places to raise seed. The company went broke after two years, and Lester was its receiver.

Lester was urged to run for Okanogan County Commissioner. He ran as a Democrat, but received a good deal of help from his fine friends, George Zahn and Leroy Wright, who took him on their Republican caravan through the county. He was elected, and he and Ethel moved back to Winthrop.

While Lester was a commissioner, the county got out of debt and built a much-needed addition to the county courthouse. He was a conscientious and popular commissioner and ran for a second term. During his 12 years in office, from 1941 to 1953, Lester and Ethel sold their ranch and used much of their own savings to make ends meet, but they felt good about doing public service.

The Otto Bernbeck family bought the Hollaway place in 1946. The Bernbecks had been living in Twisp since 1931 and were well acquainted with Lester, who sold the ranch to them with no down payment. Otto raised potatoes and pigs and built a 120-foot-long potato cellar on the property. Other than the new cellar, the place stayed about the same until 1950, when Otto traded it for a place in Snohomish and the family moved away.

To complete the Hollaway story, it is important to note that on Aug. 22, 1972, Lester and Ethel, both 85 years old, celebrated their 64th wedding anniversary. That September the North Cascades Highway opened. This was an event Lester had worked a lifetime to celebrate. He was chosen to cut the ribbon that started the caravan of cars over the highway, and he rode with Washington State Governor Dan Evans. It was greatly satisfying for Lester and Ethel to participate in this event and to see the plaque on the side of the road with Lester's name listed along with those of Jack Abrams, Morris Bolinger, Leonard Therriault and George Zahn, who also did so much to make the highway a reality.

Lester died in 1973 at age 86; Ethel died three years later at age 89. Both are buried at Sullivan Cemetery in Winthrop.

The Looney family suffered a tragedy in 1932 when Will dropped dead of a heart attack while herding sheep. He was only 49 years old. He left his wife Olive and two young children. Olive moved the family to Heckendorn to live next door to her parents. She died in 1965 at age 83 and is also buried at Sullivan Cemetery. Fred Patterson, who was married to Will's sister and lived next door, took over the Looney ranch after Will's death.

Angus McLeod

In 1918, Angus McLeod homesteaded HES 113, which was a 114-acre piece of land down valley about a half mile east of the Mazama Bridge. Angus was born in Glengary, Canada, and came to the Okanogan Valley in the early 1890s to seek his fortune in the mines. He was a skilled workman and furniture maker. Angus built his home in the pines of Mazama, where he lived for 29 years. He also constructed a commercial building that housed a store, post office and accommodations for room and board. He was postmaster for 12 years, until his death in 1928. Years later the neglected building fell down.

Angus also owned a spot on the river, next to the Mazama bridge, that was just right for picnics. It was used as a community gathering area, complete with an outdoor dance floor. The site was the scene of many gala Fourth of July celebrations. Just down the road was a good-sized clearing that became the first official Mazama baseball field.

Games hosted by the Mazama home team included contests with Winthrop, Robinson, Rock View and Twisp. Today, hopeful rodeo riders gather to test their skills on the old ballfield.

Alva and Selma Welch

The story of the Alva Welch family is an appropriate one to include at this point, not because of any earthshaking event, but because their story is so typical of the early Mazama settlers.

Gordon Welch, who was a baby when his dad moved the family here to homestead, shared the following memories of his early life in the Early Winters area.

As was the case with many settlers on the Pacific Coast, Alva Welch had been a Midwest farmer, in Iowa. He moved to Seattle, where he got involved in the building trade. Gordon was born Aug. 19, 1911. The following year, Alva moved his wife Selma and three boys, Irvin, Lawrence, and baby Gordon, to Mazama, where he built a house above Early Winters Creek on HES 91. (The house later became part of the Shafer ranch and is still referred to as the "Rattlesnake House.")

The "Rattlesnake House," formerly known as the Welch house, was moved to what would have been a golf course fairway under one proposal for development at Early Winters. Today it is part of a conservation easement and home to a rare bat colony.

Alva was a craftsman and the house he built had special features such as siding, bay windows, and detailed woodwork – finishing touches most other homes lacked. Alva's talents were in great demand, and since the Mazama economy of the time was pretty much based on the barter system, he mostly was paid in goods and services, not cash.

The community's original road ran right in front of the Welch house on the north side. The barn was to the west. A spring and shallow well were across the road and down the bank about 100 feet. All household water was hauled from there, and milk was cooled in the spring. The Welches had about a dozen cows. They fed milk to their pigs and sold cream once a week to get a few dollars for spending money.

They could sell their cream in two spots in Winthrop – at the cheese maker's place down by the bridge, or at the Okanogan Creamery. The creamery used the feed store next to the bank as a pickup point. If cheese sales were not very good, the cheese maker didn't buy cream, and sometimes the feed store wouldn't take it, either. When this happened, the Welches had to take their cream all the way to Twisp to sell it. Between logging, building, and keeping a dozen or so cows, Alva managed to make a living.

The years passed and Gordon started school. It was a long walk to Goat Wall where, for a few years, the one-room log school was located. In mid-winter, Gordon walked through snow packed down on the trail and frozen firm by zero-degree temperatures. By late winter and spring, temperatures rose a bit by afternoon, and by the time the children began their walk home from school, the snow had begun to melt. This made for an awful struggle for Gordon and his young friends because their short little legs broke through the snow crust. By this time of year, Gordon couldn't wait for the snow to be gone.

Selling cream was a primary source of income for early valley farmers. This ad regularly appeared in the Methow Valley Journal.

The school at Goat Wall existed for only a few years. A larger, more permanent school (today's Mazama Community Club) was built near the bridge across the river on a piece of ground owned by Ed Kagle. The move shortened Gordon's daily trip a bit and allowed him more time to help out at home. The move probably also made for more regular school attendance.

Gordon recalled the Indians at Early Winters when he was a child. Between 100 and 150 Indians would come to Mazama in late summer. They came on horses with their entire families, carrying their possessions in large woven baskets. They made camp at the confluence of Early Winters Creek and the Methow River, about where the Early Winters Campground is today.

The Indians carried beautiful, tapered three-prong spears to catch salmon. While the men were fishing, the women and children walked up Early Winters Creek picking berries. The men built large racks out of logs and smoked fish and the women mixed berries with fish to make a paste called pemmican.

The mining boom was generally over by the teens, but a small number of mines were still being worked and individual prospectors were plentiful. The Welch family became acquainted with one old-timer who came through the area every year. He was a typical prospector, complete with pick and shovel, a donkey, a dog and a .38 revolver on his hip. He stopped to visit the Welches before moving on, but would never tell where he was digging. Apparently he would mine each summer and make enough money to live well in Seattle for the rest of the year.

One year, after the prospector left the house, Alva noticed two men on horseback following the old fellow. The miner didn't go far before he camped that evening because he had spent a lot of time visiting the Welches. He built a fire and settled down for the night. But long before the two men were aware of it, the old miner vanished, giving them the slip.

Mazama dairy farmers took their cream to Winthrop. This photograph of the Winthrop Creamery includes manager Al Haase.

The miner stopped by the Welches a few more springtimes on his way into the mountains. When he came out in the fall, he always stayed at the Winthrop Hotel. One morning he didn't come down for breakfast. The manager eventually went up to his room and found the old miner dead in bed with a sack of gold nuggets under his pillow.

Selma Welch died in 1929 and the men left the ranch a short while later to settle in the Seattle/Everett area. Charlie Woods agreed to look after their place and care for the stock in exchange for being allowed to cut and keep the hay. That winter, a couple of big storms hit. One night, four feet of snow fell on top of what already was there and the barn roof collapsed, breaking the back of the saddle horse. Charlie let the team go. They ran down valley, and unattended, starved to death.

Dennis and Ellen Overturf

Dennis Overturf, from Badger Mountain in the Wenatchee area, staked a claim on HES 93, not quite a mile up the trail from the Welch place. By the winter of 1914, he had completed enough of the house that his wife Ellen and their newborn son Vernon could move in, but there was so much snow they spent the winter in Twisp, where they had been living while Dennis staked the homestead and worked on the house. The road went along the bank behind the house, around the barn that sat on a little flat, and then on up valley to HES 94. There was a path down by the fruit cellar, behind the small separator house.

The family raised some hay and kept a few cows. Dennis, who became the biggest farmer in the area, built a ditch from the Methow River that extended well over a mile upriver to supply water for both HES 93 and HES 92. Building a ditch to the proper grade through rocky soil with a one-horse scraper and moving huge boulders by hand was hard work. Dennis used great quantities of blasting powder and eventually got the job done.

He was a hard worker who also sold some timber to the Fender Mill by the Weeman Bridge, but he spent a lot of time cutting cedar on Early Winters Creek to make fence posts. He would haul these to Winthrop and sell them for 12 to 15 cents apiece. He also was a musician who played the guitar and violin at dances along with Calloway Cassal, who played guitar and banjo.

Homestead life was rough for the family, particularly during the cold winters. In fact, the snow was so deep when Dennis's daughter Merle was born in February of 1917 that she had to be delivered by Dennis and his neighbor Selma Welch because the doctor was unable to make it to the house.

The Dennis Overturf homestead house during a typical Mazama winter. The land was later owned by members of the Short family, who occupied it until it was purchased by Don and Dorothy Shafer in 1945. The Shafers sold it to investors in the proposed ski area.

When Vernon was old enough to go to school, he had to ford either the Methow River or Early Winters Creek. He usually crossed the Methow and went to the Mazama School along the road under Goat Wall. He generally rode his horse, but in winter it was very difficult for Vernon and his sister to get to school. The neighbors had built the small, one-room Goat Wall School on HES 94 for the few families living in the area. (When the larger school by the bridge was finished, the "neighborhood" school was no longer used and the Overturfs moved down valley for the winter.)

During several winters, the Overturf family moved into Angus McLeod's building in Mazama. The post office was on the right side of the building and the store on the left. Upstairs there were a number of rooms, along with quarters for the proprietor. The Overturfs kept their cows out back near the milking barn. Ellen, Vernon's mother, cooked for the boarders, mostly bachelor miners working various small mines and claims in the Mazama area.

The Overturfs also lived in what had been the post office building a mile down river from the Mazama bridge, probably the Way house. Another winter, they lived in Winthrop in the back of the feed store next to Simon Shafer's grocery store (today's Emporium).

The best arrangement, however, was when they leased the Cooper place in Rock View. This was a good farm with lots of land and a good place to keep the Overturf cows in winter. George Cooper had a business out of the valley, so leasing the farm to Dennis was quite convenient. Cooper visited the farm frequently and always remained interested in the place.

When Dennis Overturf died in the late summer of 1929 at age 40, Carl Weller, a good friend of Dennis and George Cooper, stepped in to help run the farm. Carl was a logger for the Fender Mill and he had been helping with the milking prior to Dennis's death.

Bad luck continued for the rest of the Overturfs after Dennis's death and also for the Coopers. One weekend when George Cooper and his son were visiting the farm, they and Carl Weller decided to set out a group of apple trees. They came up with the idea that instead of hand-digging holes to plant the trees, they would use dynamite. They set a number of charges, lit the fuse and went inside to have lunch. They counted the charges as they went off, and by the time lunch was over, all but one had blown. When Carl went to investigate, the remaining charge blew and killed him.

After that, Vernon's mother had to sell the cows. With both Dennis and Carl gone, the family could no longer manage farm tasks. They moved into the Holcomb house. At the time, Vernon was in the eighth grade, living with an aunt and going to school in Waterville. He was a man in many ways, but still unable to make a living to support his family.

Vernon lived in Pateros his sophomore year of high school. He worked for the Forest Service and pitched hay for 25 cents an hour. Before he finished high school, he lived in the back of the bakery in Pateros and would start work baking at 3 a.m. Summers he worked for the Forest Service. He became a partner in the bakery while still in high school. Sometime after graduation, he worked on Grand Coulee Dam.

Meanwhile, his mother took in a couple of teachers as boarders, but that didn't result in much of an income. After a few years, their debts were too great. The family could no longer pay the taxes on the ranch in Mazama and lost it in a tax sale. The farm was purchased by their neighbors and eventually was occupied by Edith Short.

Ellen Overturf remarried in 1936 to Robert Dunbar, a Pateros banker and orchardist.

Bill and Ella Wehmeyer

Members of the Wehmeyer family homesteaded a considerable number of acres in the upper Methow Valley and played a major role in the growth and future of the Mazama area. The first to arrive was William H. (Bill) Wehmeyer, who left Pasco, Washington,

William Wehmeyer built this house at the turn of the last century. His son Jack lived there later, and in 1996 the house was completely renovated.

in 1892 and struck out to find his fortune and a homestead in the Methow. He found the spot he was looking for six miles northwest of Winthrop at what would come to be known as Rock View. Bill cut trees, cleared land, and built a cabin. By 1894, he had talked his wife Ella into joining him on the homestead.

Ella rode for seven days in a four-horse rig with a baby on her lap to her new home. Her husband's brother, Fred Wehmeyer, drove the wagon through Coulee City. They ferried across the Columbia River, then traveled down Texas Creek to Silver, which was mostly washed out in the floods of that year.

Bill and Ella had five sons: Ray, who died as a young man; Harley, who settled HES 81; Lou, who built on the lower part of HES 81; Charlie, who settled a homestead west of his father's place; and Jack, who took over his father's homestead farm.

Bill's brother Fred claimed HES 180, a 34-acre parcel east of the Weeman Bridge. Bill's brother-in-law, H.H. (Hank) Johnson, took a homestead next to Charlie's place.

About 1900, Hank and Bill set up a sawmill by the road just below the house. This led to Wehmeyer domination of the Rock View community. The mill probably supplied the lumber sold at Guy Waring's Methow Trading Company.

After growing up in Rock View, Harley Wehmeyer moved up valley to Mazama, where

William and Ella Wehmeyer.

William Wehmeyer built a fine barn that was such a tourist attraction it was listed as an historic building in the 1980s, which meant Highway 20 had to be constructed to preserve it. However, the heavy snow of 1995-6 took it down.

he established his homestead in 1909. After clearing a few acres and building a shack, he married Bertha Vidger, from Athol, Idaho, who had come to Rock View to visit her sister and brother-in-law. Bertha's sister ran the cook shack at the Rockview Sawmill and her brother-in-law worked there. Bertha stayed on to help her sister, and in 1910, she met Harley. They were married the same year. Although they moved into Harley's shack, they started at once to build a new house that would be their home in Mazama for the next 54 years.

Harley worked at clearing land to raise hay for his horses and about 30 head of dairy cows. He particularly liked horses, and was a packer of some note. He packed for Hazard Ballard out of Lost River and for the U.S. Forest Service. He also was head packer for the 1933 North Cross State Highway survey team. Along with packing came the work of building back country trail. The Pasayten Wilderness was part of Harley's world and was as familiar to him as the trails and hills between Winthrop and Mazama where he grew up.

The William Wehmeyer house today.

Mazama's main street circa 1920s. On the left is the Mazama Store, operated by Homer and Lucille Peters, with living quarters added on the side. The building, without the living quarters, has been moved several times. It became part of the Mazama Ranch House complex and later was the Burnt-finger BBQ. The two-story building in the center is gone but may have been the Bertrum place and a one-time post office. The white building in the distance was at one time a school house. Today it is the Mazama Community Club, which is painted red.

Chapter 4

The 1920s
Improvements and New Arrivals

Many of the exciting and noteworthy events that occurred in the area during the 1920s were recorded in the *Methow Valley Journal*. For example, on July 24, 1924, the *Journal* began its 13th year of publication with the headline: "Twisp Entire Business Section Burned Last Night." Although no lives were lost, at least 17 buildings were reduced to a pile of ashes by the time the fire, which started at Dr. Holmes office, was over.

In the same issue, the paper recalled that the two most important events in Winthrop's rapidly growing prosperity were the installation of the electric light and power plant, followed by the incorporation of the Town of Winthrop.

A note in the August 14, 1924, edition of the paper reported that "Dr. E.P. Murdock, Winthrop's highly esteemed young physician and surgeon, is altering his hospital to make room for two additional beds, making five in all." Dr. Murdock arrived in Winthrop April 6 and now, just over four months later, had performed nearly 40 major operations, the paper said.

That same summer, Elbert Cassal started ed promoting his Winthrop – Mazama Stage, which ran Mondays, Wednesdays and Fridays by "Auto Speed Truck." The timbers were replaced on the Goat Creek Bridge and the Mazama Bridge was "tightened," undoubtedly a comfort to Elbert on his stage runs hauling passengers, freight and mail.

The Cassal family is mentioned throughout this book. Elbert's parents were Joshua and Charity Sloane Cassal, who are related to many of Mazama's early citizens. The Cassal and Sloane families came west in the same railroad car from Kentucky, eventually arriving in the Methow Valley in 1909. The Cassals had eight children, six of whom were born in Kentucky. Their third child, Calloway, is of particular note in the history of Mazama.

Elbert Cassal announced his "auto speed truck" stage service between Winthrop and Mazama in an advertisement published in an August 1924 issue of the Methow Valley Journal.

Calloway Cassal

The son of a homesteader who claimed his own homestead, HES 198, at age 22, Calloway married Rosa May James of Wenatchee. Their place was at the bottom of Driveway Butte on the west side of the Methow River at the end of the valley. The land was beautiful and the views stunning, but it was difficult land to farm and the winters were severe.

Over the years Calloway acquired more land, built a mile of ditch and irrigation flume, installed miles of deer fence and built barns and other outbuildings. He raised Hereford cattle on his ranch, which he called the C Bar C, and in 1964 was named "Farmer of the Year." The Cassals retired to Ephrata in 1965 after selling the farm. The new owners rented the house, which had been built by Calloway with trusses ordered

The Mazama Post Office in the 1920s.

from a Sears Roebuck catalog, to various tenants and the land was farmed and grazed over the next few decades, but it never again was the flourishing storybook ranch that Calloway built.

The house stood until May 2007. It had been empty for years, except for a number of rock chucks, mice and other critters. The owner looked into moving it, but the permit process and expense were troublesome. Instead, it was burned down.

Driving Logs and Sheep

Logging was prospering in Mazama in the 1920s. The Rockview Mill had closed, but the Goat Wall Mill owned by Peters & Sons, and the Fender Mill near the Weeman Bridge, were operating. During one spring drive at the Fender Mill, it was reported that "A million feet of logs were moving toward the mill where booms are ready to divert them into the mill pond. The drive lasts for days and there is much interest in the valley in the drive's success." A steady stream of cars made the loop between the Weeman Bridge and Mazama to see the floating logs.

Large sheep drives also were a feature of valley life in the 1920s and 1930s. Cattle replaced sheep in later years, but in the early 1920s sheep were big business. Sheep herding generally was done by stockmen from outside the valley, while the cattle people were local. Sheep were grazed from the Columbia River to the Canadian border, following the mountain ridges on both sides of the Methow valley. The drive routes went right up along the crests and ridges, down the river drainage and up the other side to back-country valleys. These drives lasted all summer.

Grazing sheep through this beautiful country might sound like an ideal summer outing, but in reality it was a tough and rugged way to make a living. Constant supervision was needed, and even then the losses were often significant. A 1921 Forest Service report estimated the following losses among 11 sheep outfits:

150 lost to poisonous plants

60 killed by wolves or coyote

35 killed by bear

500 strayed

While these losses were out of nearly 30,000 sheep, the numbers were nonetheless considered high.

Grizzly Bear and Cougar

The Aug. 30, 1923, edition of the *Methow Valley Journal* carried the first of a number of stories about government hunter P.C. Peterson, who had tracked down a grizzly bear that had been killing cattle. "Mr. Peterson trailed him through the Holman Pass into Whatcom County, where he succeeded in killing him. He was a monster, a stout man not being able to lift his hide."

The grizzly weighed 1,360 pounds and reportedly slaughtered 35 head of cattle and 150 sheep. Starting at Robinson Creek, cattle had been killed on range land in the Yellow Jacket, Goat Creek and Lost River areas. The kills had been attributed to cougars and common bears until one night W. R. Flourney, the range boss, heard a commotion and bellowing cow in distress. He investigated in the moonlight and saw an enormous bear hugging a full grown cow and eating her alive. Mr. Flourney was armed with only a revolver. He opened fire, driving the bear away, then killed the fatally wounded cow. He also notified the cattlemen and government hunter Peterson.

Government hunter Pete Peterson poses with the hide of an enormous grizzly bear he tracked and shot in 1923 at the headwaters of Ruby Creek. The bear had killed cattle on the Yellow Jacket, Goat Creek and Lost River grazing ranges outside Mazama.

One month later, on Sept. 30, 1923, the *Journal* claimed that Peterson had bagged the only true grizzly ever killed in Washington. "There have been many big bears killed that were supposed to be grizzly, but the true grizzly has a peculiar ridge of bone on the skull that distinctly marks him," the story said.

The following year, in early October, 1924, the paper reported that Peterson and his wife showed up in Winthrop to get re-supplied. Peterson said he was about a week behind another big stock-killing grizzly bear. He lost its track near "Falls country," and since he was low on supplies, he left his bear hounds at Billy Robinson's place at Lost River and headed into town.

In Winthrop, Peterson heard the bear had scattered 150 sheep on the Lost River range. This news made possible a new plan of attack. He would not go directly there, but rather would strike farther north through Windy Pass. If that plan failed, he and his party would head for Granite Mountain country, on the theory that the grizzly might follow the sheep in that direction. There was no further word on his efforts.

In November, about a month after that grizzly bear incident, a big cougar made his appearance at the J.A. Cassal ranch. Peterson, Roma Johnson and Ed Ramm took up his trail. But according to the newspaper, the cougar "made his getaway."

On Christmas Day, 1924, the *Methow Valley Journal* reported that a cougar had killed 14-year-old James Fehlhaber 10 miles west of Okanogan. The young man (actually two months shy of his 14th birthday) had been on his way to borrow a team of horses when he took a shortcut through a snowy canyon and was fatally attacked as he ran along.

Fear and feelings ran high. There were cougar stories in the paper almost every week from January until June. The Rock View news section included the following item on January 15, 1925: "Since the cougar excitement there are more dogs at our school than pupils, as each one has from one to four dogs. So Mr. Cougar better hide out."

The paper carried story after story about what became an emotional debate because two cougars were killed, with claims that seemed to support each as the murderous animal. That saga is well documented in Bruce A. Wilson's book, "Late Frontier, A History of Okanogan County, Washington."

At the height of interest in cougars one newspaper office started selling postcards of what it called the dead "Boy Killing Cougar."

However frightened the citizenry, social life went on despite cougars and bears. For example, a dance at the Rock View Hall given by the Mt. McKinney School was a great success, raising $107 toward the purchase of an organ for the school.

Road Improvements

January and February of 1925 produced some heavy snowfalls. A common practice was for families to meet for Sunday dinner and for the men to plow snow. Will Haase and W.H. Wehmeyer plowed out the road from Winthrop to the mill at Rock View with eight horses. The Feb. 5 issue of the paper said, "The people of Rock View want to thank Dr. Murdock for the interest he took in helping them V the roads. He hired a man and team, and they sure needed them before we were through."

Plowing was accomplished by pulling a wooden "V" through the snow. The "V" was constructed with two planks, three inches thick, about 23 inches wide, and about 20 feet long. Heavy hinges allowed the "V" to be set at various widths. Roads in Twisp were plowed by a "V" pulled by a 1918 Army truck. Mazama residents used two or more teams of horses and each resident would pull the "V" along their section of the road.

A bridge across Lost River, built by the Forest Service and finished in 1928, was another important improvement essential to the development of the Slate Creek district. Before the bridge existed, it was necessary to ford Lost River. Sometimes, the river was too high to cross safely.

The Forest Service had established Methow Camp Resort two miles beyond the bridge at Robinson Creek. The plan was for the camp to become one of the state's most popular spots for campers, fishermen and tourists, since it was only 20 miles from Winthrop with good road all the way.

The road west of Mazama was improved during the 1920s. It followed along the riverbank, past the old school, then ran in front of the

Those who live in Mazama have been using skis for work and play for decades. Here Ed Kagle, Harvey Dunham and Guy Sharp take a break. Circa 1920s

future Early Winters Ranger Station. The road continued across Early Winters Creek past the Cassal place and on to the Arnold homestead on McGee Creek.

The 1920s brought more change to area schools. The Mazama school was moved from the Arnold's log house on HES 84 to a building on HES 114 near the McLeod Hotel. The state legislature appropriated $360 for an additional log school at Goat Wall on Calloway Cassal's place. The appropriation provided a $60 monthly salary for a teacher, and Mildred McDermott was chosen. Mildred was the daughter of Fred McDermott, a well-known man who ran steamboats on the Columbia River. She boarded with Mrs. Short and rode her horse to school each day.

In the spring of 1925, the *Journal's* Mt. McKinney news section reported, "Owing to Fred Patterson's ill luck (his wife's health problems) the Mazama Grange has decided to set aside Tuesday April 21st to donate a day's work or money to help him out. Anyone wishing to help with team or single handed is invited ... The ladies will serve dinner at Harley Wehmeyer's." The event was a big success. Ten teams and 17 men worked at clearing, plowing, harrowing and re-seeding, plus $15 was collected.

Daily mail service started in Mazama in 1928, the same year the Star Route between Winthrop and Mazama was extended to include the west side of the river from the Weeman Bridge to Mazama.

The dream of a cross-state road continued in the 1920s. The local commercial clubs drew attention to the need by holding an annual pilgrimage to Cascade Pass. In the summer of 1928, the *Journal* announced the Twisp Commercial Club was organizing the third such pilgrimage along with clubs from Okanogan, Chelan and Pateros.

Each year an additional stretch of road was being graded and paved from the west side. However, no road was being built down the east side of the mountains to Lake Chelan, or up Bridge Creek to drop into the Methow Valley.

Methow citizens felt such a road was the key to the valley's future. If the county and community didn't bring it about, the citizens would have to wait for the state to build down from the other side, and nobody knew how long that would take. The road would serve the double purpose of providing a route for visitors and sightseers, and of establishing an outlet for the mineral and chemical resources found in this promising territory. The campaign for such a road had been going on for 33 years, ever since the road was started in 1895.

The 1920s also brought new families to the area. Their stories, some of which are shared here, are both interesting and typical of those who arrived during this period.

Bert Boughey

In 1919, Bert Boughey claimed HES 95, a 132-acre chunk of land four miles west of Mazama just above Gate Creek on the road to Robinson. He built a log house and cleared a cedar forest to make room for a garden. As the years went by, the amount of land under cultivation increased very slowly. People shook their heads and said, "Boughey is more of a violin player than a farmer." But it was nice having a violin player in the community, so when H.C. Peters purchased the ranch in 1928, folks were sorry to see Bert disappear.

The only news of Bert was an occasional order for Peters, who was putting in a sawmill, or a request for someone to cut him a piece of spruce, the specifications of which he described in minute detail – thickness of tree, grain, etc. Thus locals were both pleasantly surprised and mildly astonished when half of the magazine section of a Seattle Sunday newspaper was devoted to "violin maker Bert Boughey, who is becoming famous."

Before buying HES 95 from Bert, the Peters family had a mill near the Mt. McKinney School. A ditch from the river ran to a natural little slough area that made a mill pond. Peters bought a steam engine to power his sawmill, since he planned to do more than just cut cedar posts. However, the engine's first work was to move R.E. Short's house on HES 92 (later the Shafer house) about a quarter mile east of where it originally sat to a site more convenient to the barn.

Henry and Grace Bertram

There used to be a two-story house a few hundred feet up valley from the Mazama schoolhouse. Today that spot is a trailhead parking area, but the indentation and stones that were the foundation of Henry and Grace Bertrams' home on HES 114 still can be seen.

Henry Bertram was born in Germany and came to America at age five. He first lived in Arizona, where his father was killed by Indians. As a young man he worked on cattle ranches and spent a year driving a 20-mule team for the Borax plant in Death Valley.

After hearing about the Northwest, he rode his horse to Washington state in 1903 and spent the winter on the Okanogan River.

At 26, he married Grace Alexander in Brewster. The couple lived in a log cabin, had seven children and farmed a dryland homestead, which went fine until the drought years came. One season things were so bad the grain grew less than six inches high. In 1928, the Bertrams log cabin burned down and they lost most of their belongings.

In August of 1928, Henry and Grace and the three youngest children – Martha, Ellen, and Stanley – moved to Mazama. Grace ran the post office, and Henry farmed land they apparently had bought from Ed Kagle. Martha and Stanley milked cows at their farm and made some money milking for neighboring farmers. But the family still couldn't make it. Henry and Grace lost the farm and moved back to Brewster. Martha later married Paul Heaton of Winthrop, whom she met at a dance in Mazama.

Ed Kagle probably got the farm back and sold it to Bob Stookey in the late '30s. Bob farmed it alone until he suffered a foot injury. His brother Allan and his wife Grady then joined him.

The Sloane family settled in Mazama in the early 1900s. Shown, left to right, are Selma, Tom, Walt, Mary Jane and Tom Sloane.

The Sloanes and Stewarts

Nancy Sloane, a widow with seven children and several grandchildren, left Kentucky by rail in 1908 with all the family's belongings. She eventually homesteaded in Mazama on land with nice timber and level ground, situated on a stretch of river that didn't appear to flood frequently. Nancy's son Tom filed a claim on HES 202, which is now part of the Frank Kline and Doug Devin ranches. Nancy filed upriver on HES 200, part of which is the Burkhart Ranch today. Tom later purchased the homestead from her and added to the larger Sloane ranch. Tom's brother Robert filed a claim down valley about a mile. Tom and Robert were farmers, loggers and builders and they both hacked their ranches out of the wilderness.

Martha Sloane was one of Nancy's 10 grandchildren. Daughter of Tom, she was born in Kentucky in 1906, and was two years old when Nancy and crew settled in Mazama. Martha grew up with all the trials and joys of frontier living. She walked several miles down valley along a tree-lined road and over a narrow bridge across Little Boulder Creek to the one-room Mt. McKinney School.

Young Martha Sloane looked forward to social events both in Mazama and, on special occasions, in Winthrop. The Fourth of July was a major event in the early West, and Winthrop celebrated in typical style with picnics, ball games and dances. It was at one of these events that Martha met Bill Stewart, her future husband.

Actually, Martha met two young men on that Fourth of July, and when she received a letter from one of them a few days later she didn't remember which one he was. She was 16 years old at the time, but by the time she turned 18 and married Bill Stewart, she had sorted things out.

Bill was five years older than Martha. Born in 1901, he came to the Methow in 1922. Bill and Martha were married in Wenatchee in 1924 and started keeping house in a building just down river from the Weeman Bridge. Bill spent three years working for the mill as yard man. He was one of 26 men with their own teams who hauled logs in the winter of 1929 when the temperature reached 47 degrees below zero. Some of the working horses died that winter and Bill guessed that they died of frozen lungs from breathing hard.

 One interesting observation made by Martha in later years was about the trees and foliage on Sandy Butte, the mountain behind her house. As a small girl she recalled seeing cattle grazing on a sparsely treed hillside. Today, the same hillside is thickly forested with trees 60 to 80 years old. Because there were no known fires or previous logging, speculation is that the area must have undergone a climate change.

In 1927, Bill and Martha obtained 40 acres of land from Martha's father, Tom Sloane. Only three trees had been cut on the entire place. Bill went to work clearing most of the land. He sold logs to the mill and bought back lumber to build his house and barn, which took about three years to complete. The house became one of the showplaces of Mazama because of Martha's talent for gardening. Bill bought eight dairy cows from Lester Hollaway and, like nearly everyone else, went into the dairy business.

Other homesteaders followed the same general practice by raising some cows, sheep and chickens. Bill remembers that the Weeman family had a homestead that spanned the river above the Fender Mill on the north side of the river. Weeman had a patch of red clover and a few cows, but he also had a different product than most. Weeman had 100 to 150 black cats and sold the skins for up to $3 apiece to a fur company. The winter the two horses died from the cold at the mill, Weeman dragged the carcasses up to his place and the cats fed on horsemeat most of the winter. Weeman also had a little wagon and would travel to where people were butchering and collect scraps to feed the cats.

Bill Stewart left the valley in 1927 to mine in Kellogg, Idaho. He returned and logged or trapped every year until 1944. His traps were set in Little Boulder, Fawn and Ramsey creeks. Trapping started in the creek bottom, where Bill would get 15-18 mink. When the creek froze, the mink left, so he trapped farther up for marten. He would get about the same number of marten. He also made a long trip on snowshoes up to the headwaters of Huckleberry Creek, making his last trip for the season during the first part of January.

Bill also worked at clearing the right-of-way for power lines to the uppermost reaches of the valley. Electricity was made possible by the Rural Electrification Administration, a federal government program started under President Franklin D. Roosevelt's second New Deal. The REA, which still exists today, subsidized electricity to rural areas that were not served by private power companies. Land for the power lines was mostly dedicated for public use by property owners.

Edgar Hotchkiss was Bill's boss. Besides being an electrician, Edgar was a miner in the Mazama area with diggings along Goat Wall and Flag Mountain. Like nearly everyone in the area, he had to have several skills to get by in Mazama.

Martha's sister, Selma Sloane, married Earl Short, who had farmed HES 92, and they lived on the Overturf homestead, HES 93.

Martha's youngest brother, Walter, was born in Mazama and returned after World War II. He and his brother Tom bought the Sloane ranch.

Karl and Auguste Wickert

The Karl Wickert family had a homestead next to Nancy Sloane's place. Karl was a fine old German craftsman who built a nice house for his family. He constructed buildings throughout the Mazama area for many years and completed such area landmarks as the large barn for the Kumm family in the McKinney Mountain area.

Karl and Auguste Wickert gave acreage to their daughters, Marie and Frieda. Marie married a fellow named Beryl Crawley, who built a house on Little Boulder Creek about 50 feet from the present Highway 20, on a site that now is near the front gate of the Devin ranch. Beryl built a root cellar in the bank of an old creek wash and raised some chickens. Marie planted a garden and put flowers around the house. A wagon road and a bridge over the creek ran south of the house, toward Sandy Butte. The Crawleys didn't stay long at the property, however, and the place changed hands several times. Eventually, it was purchased by E.A. and Grace Arbuckle, the neighbor to the west.

Mr. Arbuckle was one of the first serious farmers in the area. He cleared land, worked up the soil, put in a five-acre orchard south of the Crawley house and planted 50 acres of peas on HES 202. He had problems with both crops, problems familiar to Mazama residents. The growing season was too short for fruit trees, plus the deep snow and deer broke down their tender branches. The peas grew well but the deer discovered them at the flowering stage and again when the pods were ripe. From 800 feet away the neighbors could hear the "pop, pop, pop" of pea pods as the deer munched through a big part of the crop.

Being more than a little unhappy about the deer intrusion, the farmer complained to the game warden, George McDaniels. George didn't have a ready answer, but in a few days he gave Arbuckle three boxes of shells with the warning, "Don't cripple 'em."

Dr. J.W. Malzacher owned the place after Arbuckle and either he or Arbuckle decided they had no use for the Crawley house. The community needed a church and Sunday school building, so the Crawley house was donated to this worthy cause and moved across the creek and about a half mile down valley to a site donated for the purpose. The building was painted and kept in good repair by the ministers. It never had water or a sewer, so the children used two outhouses. A big wood stove heated the building, either too much or too little, but Sunday school went on.

Marie Wickert's sister Frieda married Tom Davis and later Tim Wilmurth. Frieda had a house, garden and chicken coop about 300 yards east of Little Boulder Creek. Evidently, Frieda was not the easiest person to get along with, although she liked horses and kept some on the property. This greatly irritated her second husband Tim. They had no pasture, so Tim had to buy feed, which they could ill afford. This apparently led to a number of arguments between Frieda and Tim, one of which culminated with Tim announcing that he was going to kill himself. He marched out of the house carrying his hunting rifle and went across the snow to the fruit cellar about 30 feet away. The next sound Frieda heard was the discharge of the rifle.

It was Sunday morning and snowing. She put on her coat and overshoes and went directly to Walt Stout's house across the road. She told Walt she thought Tim might have killed himself. Walt went to the nearby church, which was conducting services, and enlisted Bill Stewart to go with him to investigate. Their worst fears were confirmed. Tim had put the rifle in his mouth and pulled the trigger.

Walt and Bill were careful to note that only one set of tracks led to the cellar. Bill called the sheriff and the evidence appeared to clear Frieda of any guilt, although some in the area whispered their suspicions that she had done it. She did go to the cellar after the body was removed and carefully washed and wiped all the jars that had been splattered with blood and flesh. This was regarded by a few as a cold and unsympathetic gesture that only confirmed their theory about who actually killed Tim.

Matilda, the third Wickert sister, married Rowe Strausbaugh. They lived next to her parents. Strausbaugh bought HES 202 and lived in the house that stood by the road until taken out by the new road in the mid-1980s. A shed, corral and feed bunk, now part of the Devin ranch, are all that remains.

Will Fulton

Will Fulton was six months old in 1883, when his parents and their seven other children left Decatur, Texas, in a covered wagon caravan bound for Kittitas County in the Territory of Washington. When he was 14 years old, his father died and his eldest brother, who was 17 years older than Will, became his surrogate dad.

When Will was a young man he helped his family drive their cattle over Clockum Pass and into the Methow Valley, where they found lush grass and were so impressed the family decided to buy land and settle in this "cattle heaven."

Will married Myrtle Mullin and settled on a farm in the Bear Creek area. They had five children. The second child, Lucille, was born in Twisp in 1908. She would go on to finish school in the Methow, college in Ellensburg and subsequently teach school in Mazama and Winthrop.

Lucille was in the sixth grade when her parents decided to move to Mazama. Years later she wrote about her family's adventure in a recollection titled "Our Mazama Home." Excerpts follow.

The year was 1921. On a cold, murky morning in April, we were loaded in two wagons heading for our new home thirteen miles up the south fork of the Methow River to a place called Mazama. Dad drove the lead wagon which held the old Monarch cook stove, a durable heater, our heirloom and prized possession, the old family organ, plus whatever else could be stuffed in and around these three bulky items. The second wagon, driven by my mother and my 15-year-old brother, Earl, carried the sturdy pine writing desk, the old Morris chair, Mother's much used sewing machine, her rocking chair and all the rest of our household goods. I felt so sad as I left my Bear Creek home of thirteen years but there was also a glow of excitement and adventure about going up into the forested country to live on the banks of the river.

Mother had packed a huge lunch, as this would be an all day journey. We jolted, bounced and swayed the morning away and by afternoon we were moving into mountain-ous terrain. The roads were rutty. There were patches of snow everywhere. As we drove through the gate to our new farm, about four o'clock in the afternoon, the sun had long since gone down behind the mountain that bordered our place on the west.

... the first order of business was to set to work unloading furniture. Dad set up the kitchen stove while we went to work on the beds. We retired early for there would be much to do the next day. I was lulled to sleep that night by the murmur of the flowing river. Sometime around two in the morning, we were awakened by the scream of a woman. Dad said it was a mountain lion on our west mountain welcoming us to our new home.

For a time the place was alive with activity. A huge garden, a flume to carry the excess irrigation water past our back porch, a root cellar, a cow shed and corrals all came into being. After a long busy day the milking had to be done. Dad had brought a herd of six jersey cows from Bear Creek, but I can't remember how he got them there. Perhaps he drove them ahead of our wagons when we moved.

At last the rush of getting settled and the necessary spring work was done. One evening after supper, Mother went to the organ and began to play a favorite church hymn. Before long we heard Dad's soft resonate baritone voice join in with Mother's. We three children soon joined in just as we always had and would always do as long as we remained under the same roof. We were home.

The summer went by rapidly. I enjoyed every minute of it. Before long the school bell rang again and I was back in school.

After a visit in 1997, Lucille, at the age of 89, forwarded her writings to Darrell and Marlene Ford, who owned the property and ran the Chokecherry Inn bed and break-fast. She also wrote them a letter, saying, " ... Never could I imagine that such an estab-lishment would be sitting directly on the spot where I spent my growing up years. Only the big fir tree and the remnants of the old root cellar dug in the bank of the river tells us where the log house used to stand."

Traffic at the Mazama junction of Lost River Road and Goat Creek Road in the 1930s.

Chapter 5

The 1930s
The Depression Years

While the Great Depression of the 1930s hit hard across the nation, folks in the upper Methow Valley knew it was going on but generally didn't feel the crunch. That's because nearly everyone already lived a subsistence existence as a normal way of life, so things went on about the same.

Efforts to get a road built over Cascade Pass proceeded somewhat with the award of contracts to build additional sections of road to put people to work. Interest in mining increased, perhaps because men didn't have anything else to do and had the time to prospect and promote mines. A group of Seattle and local men announced plans to open the American Flag Mine. It was reported that rich ore had been reached in the Flag Mine and that the owners had purchased part of the Angus McLeod place and were planning to put in a reduction mill.

In 1931, the post office was on HES 114, the Bertram's property. At that time, W.P. Gadeski decided to open a grocery store in Mazama and initially stored his wares in the post office building. The *Methow Valley Journal* reported that "as soon as a town site is laid out a store building will be erected." The store, built in 1936, was the second mercantile venture in Mazama. The first was in the summer of 1895 when Frank McCain set up a large tent on what became HES 203. For a few months McCain sold over the counter to miners in Mazama and Slate Creek, but he went out of business when the mining boom subsided.

Determined not to let the Depression get the better of them, the ladies of the South Fork Civic Club met and made arrangements for a "Depression Party" to be held on October 15, 1931, in the Rock View Hall. Invitations were written on wallpaper and a prize was offered for the "most amusingly dressed guest."

While the ladies planned the party, the men organized a roundup. Bob Morrow, Jack Wehmeyer, and Montray Cassal brought cows down from the Yellow Jacket range. (It was noted that the cows weren't as fat as usual.) Lots of downed timber in Black Pine Basin made the roundup difficult.

As the community of Mazama went into the winter of 1931, people felt relatively optimistic. The Fender Mill, located by the Weeman Bridge, was building a log chute in Boesel Canyon in back of Leonard Harvey's place and expected to take a season's run of logs from there through the winter. The log chute was an interesting concept that grew from the desire to take advantage of the force of gravity to move logs. The chute actually was a trench dug in the ground by teams of horses hitched to plows. Where the ditch crossed rock or ravines, it was built from logs.

To make the chute work, it was iced with water from Boesel Creek using mops and brooms. The work was done after the men already had worked a 10-hour day. By that time the temperatures had dropped. When it snowed, the chute had to be shoveled by hand with a specially shaped tool made by the blacksmith at the mill.

Logs up to 16 feet in length were skidded to the top of the chute by teams. Using peaveys, the men fed the logs into the chute. As long as everything was working properly, they slid to the bottom quickly. All too often, however, logs piled up in the chute and jumped the side, sometimes breaking apart. Logs with knots were especially difficult to get to the bottom and several men with peaveys were stationed along the chute to keep them going.

Bill Stewart, Earl Short and Tom Sloane use a Model T Ford to run a buzz saw to cut wood in the fields on Earl's place.

The logs were decked at the bottom until they could be loaded on sleds and taken to the mill, where they were again decked by the edge of the mill pond, ready for use in the spring when the mill reopened. The log chute ran for two years, but it was only marginally successful. It was also dangerous. Fortunately, only one accident occurred and that was when Paul Duffy's leg was broken while he was walking up the chute to work at the same time a log was sent down the chute prematurely.

Most men who worked on the chute lived on small farms in the area, in the mill bunkhouse, or in tar-paper cabins. The mill had a cookhouse operated by Alma Tate, who provided meals for 90 cents a day. Later in the year, the price was increased to $1.05, which caused great unrest and rumors of a strike. In the spring of 1932, the log chute was abandoned when the weather turned warm.

Another mill opened in the area. Located on HES 83, Will Looney's old place, the mill was operated by Harvey Peters and his son Ellis. Harvey had closed his Goat Wall Mill on HES 95. He and his son diverted water from Early Winters Ditch to fill the mill pond.

Dances went on throughout the winter of 1931-32 and there emerged a new group of local music makers. Calloway Cassal, Harvey Peters and Ken Fulton played for a dance at the school in December and for parties to usher in 1932.

The new year, however, brought a real sadness to Mazama when Will Looney died. He was only 49 years old and thought to be in good health. On a March day, while working sheep with Ethel Hollaway at the Hollaway ranch, he suddenly collapsed. He apparently died of a heart attack and was pronounced dead by Dr. Starr from Winthrop.

Joshua C. Cassal also died that spring. He was 60 years old and left his wife Charity, five sons and two daughters.

The snow at Early Winters could be helpful for skidding logs. Here Ray Patterson is ready for work with his team and log tongs.

Record Snow

The winter of 1934-35 was good for those who liked snow. Mazama had record snow the last week of January 1935 when 52 inches fell in 24 hours. Mazama usually got considerably more snow than Winthrop, but this same storm dumped an equal amount in Winthrop. Twisp received 30 inches and Carlton 18 inches.

Guy Waring Dies

Sad news arrived the next year. In April of 1936, the *Methow Valley Journal* reported the death of Guy Waring, founder of Winthrop, who died of a stroke at his home in Hyde Park near Boston on March 27. He had been in poor health for some time.

Waring was born in New York on January 3, 1859, son of Col. George E. Waring, Jr. He attended Harvard University and after graduating worked with his father in Newport, R.I., until 1884, when he married Helen Clarke Greene, his step-mother's younger sister, who was a widow with three children. He came west with his family to Portland,

Oregon, where they stayed a short time before buying a ranch northeast of Conconully, not far from the Canadian border.

Waring raised cattle, started a store and was one of the first Okanogan County commissioners. But by 1888 Helen wanted to "go back East to civilization," as her husband put it in *My Pioneer Past*, the book he wrote about those years. The family later came west again in 1891, this time to the Methow Valley, where Waring again started a store. On March 1, 1893, a fire consumed the whole venture. According to the *Journal's* account, Waring's bills were paid and he had $728 in the bank at the time of the fire. Because there was four feet of settled snow on the ground, the worst winter since 1862, the family could not leave the valley until May. The Warings again went East.

They returned to Winthrop in November 1897. He incorporated the Methow Trading Company, which he served as president until 1924, when mortgagees took control. In 1906, his wife died after a 10-year illness. He remarried in 1917 to the widow of George Burgess (Harvard '93), and lived in Massachusetts thereafter, the *Journal* story said.

Changes at the Fender Mill

The operators of the Fender Mill ran into trouble during the summer of 1936. A receiver was appointed and a hearing set for September. The receiver for the Fender Lumber & Box Co. appointed Martha (Gamble) Gebbers of Gamble Lumber Co. in Brewster to operate the mill for one year, from 1937 to 1938. E.E. Wagner & Son of Okanogan bought the mill and operated it for another year before moving it to Twisp. When the mill moved, it established Twisp as the commercial center of the Methow Valley.

On the bright side of the economy, reconstruction of two-and-a-half miles of road – from the state highway at the Peters Mill in Mazama to Early Winters Creek – was in progress. A 23-man detail from the Gold Creek Civilian Conservation Corps (CCC) stationed at the Early Winters administration site built the 16-foot roadbed. Ranchers helped by clearing right-of-way for the new road.

The Civilian Conservation Corps camp at Robinson. There were several CCC camps in the Methow Valley in the 1930s. The men built roads and bridges and helped fight forest fires.

U.S. Forest Service Builds at Early Winters

The Early Winters Ranger Station seemed to evolve over several years. At one point there was a CCC camp on the northwest side of the creek, but it lasted only a few months because the creek, the camp's source of water, went dry.

Cabins were built later to house specialty workers engaged in Works Progress Administration projects. They eventually were torn down. The WPA was a major government employer for federal construction projects during the Depression.

A major part of the Early Winters Ranger Station was constructed in 1937 by the WPA, which employed numerous local men. Bill Wehmeyer helped dig the basement. Walt Clark and Rowe Strasbough also worked there. George Wright was the ranger and Ray Patterson was assistant ranger. When completed, the Early Winters station became headquarters for the Pasayten District. A newly completed facility in Winthrop was headquarters for the Winthrop District.

The Pasayten was the focus of much attention, which probably is why it merited a separate ranger district. The Pasayten Airport was enlarged and completed in the summer of 1936. Building the airstrip in the wilderness was a major accomplishment. Bulldozers and equipment were taken from Barron over makeshift roads to the remote spot, then brought out again once construction was complete. Airport expansion hugely improved fire control capabilities in the area.

Early Winters was typical of the CCC's projects. The buildings had a unique architectural style and were supposed to blend with their surroundings. Rustic walls, fences and heavy, squared timbers were used. The CCC projects put fine craftsmen to work who otherwise would have had no work. The result locally was an exceptional ranger station that would one day be included on the National Register of Historic Places.

U.S. Forest Service buildings at Early Winters.

Symbols of Change

November 1937 brought a big change to Mazama when the school board voted to keep the local school closed for the winter. The projected attendance was only six students because of the 11 school-aged children, the parents of five wanted their children to go to school in Winthrop. Because it was possible to run buses, it was considered unnecessary to operate a separate school, and the state promised to keep the road open to Robinson Creek.

By the mid-to-late 1930s, Methow Valley residents had learned to enjoy their cold and snow by skiing for fun, instead of just for transportation. Ski lifts were built on Forest Service land near Patterson Mountain, and a 1,500-foot rope tow carried skiers up the slope behind Winthrop's Sunny M Ranch.

A special event called "Ski Frolic" was scheduled for March 1938 at Lewis Butte. Skiers started at First Creek in the Cub Creek drainage and

The Driveway Butte lookout. All materials were packed in by horse over steep, rugged terrain to the remote site.

had a downhill run of more than a mile back to the Methow. Mr. Kovack, a teacher in charge of the event, declared that the snow was excellent and the course steep and smooth, ensuring a very fast run. He also scheduled a "slalom or turn contest," which he felt "would be interesting for spectators and skiers alike." A Snow Queen was chosen from the high school student body. Spectators were told that the entire "frolic" could be seen from their cars.

The summer of 1938 was a dry one and the resulting fires were hard on Mazama. In July, Mr. and Mrs. R.E. Short discovered their barn on HES 93 ablaze at 4:15 in the morning. Two loads of hay were in the barn at the time. The fire spread from the barn to the separator house and then to the chicken house. All three structures burned to the ground. A CCC crew was dispatched to prevent later spot fires. Shortly after noon the same day, the Driveway Butte lookout spotted flames at the Harvey Peters house and the same CCC crew was sent in to fight that fire.

Goat Peak lookout in 1923.

Alva Sharp

A notable character in the 1930s was Guy Sharp's brother Alva, an enterprising fellow interested in mining but remembered by some for rarely wearing shoes yet being able to run over rocks with ease. Moonshine was Alva's most profitable venture during the time he kept company with Bessie Hardy, and the reliable spring above the house they shared provided an important resource. After all, a good moonshiner needs a source of good water.

Bessie and Alva Sharp's house under construction. It later burned down.

Floyd and Anna Kent

Floyd and Anna Kent stepped off the train in Pateros on March 31, 1928, and started a life that was typical of many who would inhabit the Mazama area during the next half century.

The Kents rented an upstairs apartment in Twisp, and Floyd went to work driving a lumber truck for Wetzel & Son. The work was steady until the company shut down in late fall. (At that time, road conditions limited the number of working months.)

Anna made several trips with her husband to see the country. She visited the Fender Mill above Winthrop and various orchards to deliver box material. By winter the Kents were generally familiar with the valley. Like many local people they planned to trap during the winter, so they moved to Libby Creek. Floyd went to Okanogan and bought the winter's grubstake for about $50.

The following winter the Kents left the valley to find work, but they returned in the spring. Floyd went back to driving for Wetzel and hauled logs out of Fawn Creek to the Fender Mill. They lived in one of the cabins at the mill and became acquainted with what they thought was a new and lovelier part of the valley.

When their first daughter was born, they bought property in the McKinney Mountain area from Lester

Floyd Kent built this house where his family lived for many years. The willow tree has grown and the rock chimney was added in 1975, but otherwise the house looks about the same as it did in the early '30s. Floyd also built the barn in the distance, which is a familiar landmark to those driving eastbound from Mazama on Highway 20.

Today's Mazama Community Club building started out as the last Mazama schoolhouse, which was built about 1921. A porch and kitchen were added later. This is a church group and Sunday school class that also used the building.

Hollaway. Lester had subdivided a homestead into 20-acre parcels. Floyd, who was a carpenter by trade, built a cozy, two-room house on their 20 acres just across the road from the Mt. McKinney school. The family acquired a cow, a pig and a horse to till the garden. They planted a field of grain to feed their chickens.

The Kents loved the area and their friendly neighbors. They enjoyed sleigh rides up and down the road or across the fields to the Joe Fleishman, Frank Kumm, Lester Hollaway and Bob Scott places. Everyone visited more in those days than in later years.

Anna recalled a memorable trip one winter's day when the family left home in a covered bobsled and drove all day through Elbow Canyon (now known as Elbow Coulee) and up the Twisp River to a relative's place, where they spent the night. The next day, the family drove to Carlton, spent the night at Libby Creek with friends, and then started two days travel back home again, visiting and staying with friends all along the way.

One year Helen Read, Anna's sister, came to visit and in 1931 she became the teacher at Mt. McKinney School. Helen married Bob Morrow, who was farming the Hancox homestead, and thus became a member of the community. After teaching at Mt. McKinney, Helen taught for a time in Rock View, where the school was bulging with 40 students because the Fender Mill was prospering. This was too many students for a one-room school and Miss Flint, the teacher, had a breakdown trying to cope with the challenge. Helen relieved her for the remainder of the year.

During the winter of 1934 work was hard to find. The Kents moved to Grand Coulee so Floyd could work on the dam. By the summer of 1935 they were back in the Methow enlarging their home. That was the summer they planted the weeping willow tree that still stands and has become a trademark sight on the place. Frank Kumm gave the Kents a willow switch to start the tree.

About this time the Azurite Mine was in full swing and ore trucks rumbled down

Ellis Peters, Guy Sharp, Bessie Hardy (who may have been Mrs. Alva Sharp at this time), Alva Sharp and Ed Kagle were among Mazama's movers and shakers in earlier times.

the road headed for Pateros with loads of ore that were shipped across the Cascades for processing. Floyd worked at the Azurite for a year. It was hard work and in winter the only way in or out was on snowshoes from Ed Kikendall's station at Robinson Creek.

Tight though times were, most people in the Methow felt they came through the Depression better than those in other areas. There wasn't much money in circulation, but nobody went hungry because everyone was more or less self-sustaining.

With the coming of war in the 1940s, the Kents took work in the defense industry and Floyd went to Alaska. The family was in and out of the valley for the next 10 years. Finally, in 1953, they pulled up stakes and went to Alaska. After nine years, Floyd felt it was time to turn Alaska over to the younger generation, so the Kents returned to the Methow to live out their senior years.

While Anna and Floyd retired on the Chewuch River, their daughter Elinore, who had married Don Drake, kept the family presence in Mazama by moving into the old Weeman homestead. The Weeman place had changed hands and the original house had burned, but Clarence Stout built a nice home on the original foundation. Don bought the place from Clarence and then went to work for Bill Laney and Norm Hamilton building roads and putting in utilities for the Edelweiss real estate development.

Mining in Mazama

During the summer of 1931 the promotion and opening of the Danlee Mine focused considerable attention on mining in Mazama. The mine was advertised in a 1931 *Methow Valley Journal* as the "Cow Pasture that Camouflaged Gold" and investors were solicited to buy into the lease.

There was a big promotional effort during spring and early summer culminating in a free barbecue on July 26 to celebrate shipment of the first carload of ore from the mine

out of the Methow Valley. It was reported that the largest crowd ever assembled
in Mazama attended the gala occasion.
Between 1,250 and 1,500 people showed
up and 267 cars were parked at the Danlee. Some questioned whether any ore
ever was shipped, but considerable stock
was sold that day.

The Azurite, Gold Hill, Flag and
Mazama Queen mines were operating at
that time. A store had been opened and
the *Journal* said Mazama was a thriving
farming community instead of a wilderness. According to the 1930 census, 166
persons and 35 farms were included in
the precinct. Those figures did not include people living in new homes built
during the previous year because of the
latest mining activity.

Unlike in the rest of the nation,
things seemed to be booming in Mazama during the spring of 1932. The owners of the Mazama Queen Mine near
Goat Wall Creek planned to employ 15
men for their operation. A newspaper
story said a new extraction process had
been discovered and a new company of
men from Seattle and the county had

The difficult-to-access Mazama Queen Mine, high up on Goat Wall to the southeast of Goat Wall Creek, operated on and off for some years. There are two men working in this undated photograph. Ore containing gold, silver and zinc was transported to a mill at the bottom of the wall in a basket that ran on a cableway.

been formed. They already had a compressor and drill on site and were expecting 18
tons of equipment to arrive and to be in operation by mid-May. A tunnel had been
driven a distance of 410 feet into an immense ore body and with the mine location
right on the highway a few miles from Mazama, costs for extraction were expected to
be relatively low.

However, progress did not go quite as predicted. It was June before machinery for
the electric power plant could be installed, along with an electric hoist at the head of a
tramway. After a test run it was discovered that a new type of furnace would be needed.
Despite the setbacks, a run had been made at the Mazama Queen by the end of June
with values of $80 per ton reported. Considering the price of gold was about $20 per
ounce, that was not a bad figure.

Charles Ballard – miner, engineer and designer of towns – died December 29, 1934.
But his dreams and predictions for the Slate Creek mines did not. Idle for 30 years, the
Indiana Mine came to life in 1935 under the management of owner F.D. Hyde, who
made his headquarters at the Hotel Winthrop. A small crew of men worked the site and
by September they had completed a 500-foot cableway from the mine tunnel to the floor
of the basin.

Free Barbecue

Danlee Gold Mine

at Mazama, Methow Valley, Wash.

Sunday
July 26, 1931

You are cordially invited to attend the **Big Free Barbecue and Celebration** at the Danlee Mine at Mazama. This is for the Purpose of Celebrating the

First Carload of Shipping Ore being sent out of the Methow Valley

Bring all the Family

Promotions for the Danlee Mine apparently drew the largest crowd ever assembled in Mazama to a free barbecue.

Hyde was a New York railroad construction contractor but familiar with the area. Thirty years earlier, during the Slate Creek boom, three railroads had raced their surveyors into the district. Hyde's partner and engineer directed the survey for the Canadian route up the Pasayten over Windy Pass and down Slate Creek. As a result, Parker & Hyde acquired claims on the divide. Hyde authorized a sawmill to be built and lumber was cut for a power plant and mine buildings.

In 1905, power lines had been run to Indiana Basin and to the Eureka Mill on the North Fork of Slate Creek. The Chancellor plant furnished power for two seasons, but when no railroad showed up and activities died, it was decided to patent the Chancellor holdings. Thus it was that Hyde returned years later to continue a dream that started many years earlier.

The temporary closure of the Mazama Queen Mine in March 1932 raised apprehension in the upper valley, although it was dispelled in June when it was announced that the Mazama Queen was now the Continental Gold & Silver Company. The new mine was said to be one of the best equipped plants in the Northwest despite its 50-ton capacity.

Mining as an economic factor in the local economy needs to be put into perspective. Yes, many people in the upper valley participated in mining, but frequently there was no pay. Men would work and be paid for a few weeks or months and then, when the money ran out, they would be promised stock or cash when the mine paid. The major source of revenue was from the sale of stock in the mines.

When promoters made money from stock sales the workers were paid to dig a little farther, start a new mine or reopen an abandoned or bankrupt claim. The few Mazama area mines that actually produced gold also saw any profits put back into their operation.

The Azurite, which ran all year for many years in the 1930s, was the one exception. But by 1938 even the Azurite quit. It had produced $972,000 in gold and silver, but was $120,000 short of its total investment. By 1942, owner ASARCO had removed most valuable equipment from the site.

The only men who made money from a small mine were Fred and Henry Dammann, according to Bill Wehmeyer. Henry Dammann was born in 1879 and came from Germany on a sailing ship as a young boy, like many turn-of-the-century immigrants. He started on the east coast and made his way west by working in the mines or at any other job he could find.

According to Bill, Fred and Henry had a placer mine in a creek and dug a hole and put a cabin above it. They decided to put in a root cellar by digging in the hill behind their cabin and hauling the dirt out the front door. Part way through the root cellar excavation they hit a little pocket of gold and took out about $7,000 worth. Henry eventually claimed a homestead in the Methow, but spent a big part of his gold strike profits bringing his family and relatives from Germany to America.

Highway Wrangling Continues

As dreams of prosperous mines continued, so did dreams of a North Cross State Highway. By the end of 1935, federal money was approved to build a road from Diablo to Azurite and Slate Creek. This was a significant departure from the Cascade Pass route into which so much effort and time had been invested. The decision came as a great shock to many. The federal government sent WPA crews to start a mine-to-market road from Diablo to Azurite. Whatcom County would work with the federal people to run a road up Granite Creek and the East Fork, and then over to Slate Creek. If money were available, the road would run up the existing road to the New Light Mine and over Harts Pass.

The year 1938 was just like every other year since 1890 so far as news and interest in a North Cross State Highway was concerned. The headline in the May 12 edition of the *Methow Valley Journal* said, "Ruby Cr. Road To Be Built, 1939 May See Thru Traffic To Coast By Northern Route." The pursuit of the highway was an unending battle. It was the object of countless meetings, committees, trips to the state capitol and the platform of nearly everyone running for public office in North Central Washington. The problem was not only getting the money for the highway, but also determining the route.

By the late 1930s, engineering and construction capabilities allowed roads to be built just about anywhere. Thus the location became more of a political compromise than a question of construction feasibility. The question of location remained unresolved as the 1930s came to a close.

Jack and Minnie Stewart's showplace Mazama home about 1940, before they retired to California. The main house, separator house, barn and silo can be seen beyond the flower border.

Chapter 6

The 1940s and 1950s
Cattle, Recreation, War and Flood

Beef cattle became a bigger part of the ranching scene in Mazama during the 1940s. By this time, the more persistent and harder-working farmers had begun to accumulate more land. The first generation of homesteaders was ready to retire and some of their children had left the family farm for better jobs elsewhere. This often made possible the purchase of neighboring lands at a reasonable price, and with larger pieces of land, beef cattle could be raised if a rancher also could acquire grazing rights on nearby Forest Service lands. The problem of shipping cattle to market still existed, but with improved roads and better trucks, hauling to markets as far away as Seattle became a common practice.

Albert Ventzke of Rock View an original homesteader had managed to put together three ranches totaling 360 acres. Albert and his brother Emil came to the Methow Valley the year after the area was opened for white settlement. They camped on Bear Creek. Ben Pearrygin showed them around and recommended land at the mouth of Cub Creek, where Emil Ventzke took up a claim, and in Rock View, where Albert located in 1888. The Ventzkes took the first wagons beyond the confluence of the Methow and Chewuch rivers.

Jack Stewart had put several ranches together between Goat Creek and Mazama on the north side of the river. And a number of people who had dairy herds began adding, or switching to, beef cattle. Other residents began to combine homesteads into larger tracts in the 1940s. For example, Calloway Cassal put together HES 94, 197 and 198.

Notes in the *Methow Valley Journal* in April 1941 give a flavor of what was happening in Mazama at the time:

"Andy Russell is hauling beef cattle to the Seattle Market for Paul Heaton of Winthrop, making three trips this week."

"Jack Wehmeyer took a truck load of beef cattle to Seattle this week. Mrs. Wehmeyer accompanied him."

"At roundup last fall, Calloway Cassal failed to find six head of his cattle. Since ordinarily cattle do not survive the winter on the range here he had given them up for lost but this week he found two yearlings in a protected spot at the forks of Boulder Creek. They had managed to find food enough to keep alive but were very thin. He also found the skeleton of a cow he had lost."

"Roy Kumm has installed electrical equipment in his dairy barn and separator house."

The classic Roy Kumm barn that once housed a dairy herd is currently owned by the Allison family.

New Arrivals

Don and Dorothy Shafer arrived in Mazama in the 1940s. The Shafers had been raising cattle in Edmonds, north of Seattle. At first they had dairy cows but later switched to beef cattle. However, they needed a bigger ranch if they were going to get into raising beef cattle on a major scale. Don had hunted deer in Mazama in the 1930s and it was the first place he wanted to go to expand their operation.

In 1945, the Shafers, who had purchased HES 91 sometime earlier, bought HES 92 and 93 from the Short family, giving them about 450 acres of land. Don doubled the size of the field on HES 92. He was a good mechanic, loved machinery and was one of the first in the upper valley to use a Caterpillar tractor for farming. Most Mazama farmers were using horses into the 1940s and they felt that something like a Cat was too slow. Don hooked up several discs and equipment and in one pass with the Cat did what would take many days to accomplish with a team. The next year, a number of Mazama farmers wanted to hire Don to do their field work.

The first year the Shafers lived at Early Winters, they put up hay in a mound. But the second year they got a baler and became the first ranchers in the valley to have baled hay.

New Activities

Recreation was another hot development during the 1940s. As an economic factor, recreation was expanding beyond the hunting and fishing for which the area already was noted.

On the Chewuch River, the Spaeth family opened the Methow Valley Ranch, a dude ranch that received considerable recognition. *Sunset Magazine* carried a notice that the ranch would stay open during winter to accommodate "ski dudes."

Skiing grew in popularity during the 1940s. The season of 1940-41 had been a glorious one for snow and enthusiasm was high. The Forest Service and Civilian Conservation Corps constructed a ski hill with a rope tow on the mountainside southwest of

Patterson Lake that was within easy driving distance of upper Methow Valley towns.

During January and February, 560 names were recorded in the registry at the warming hut at the bottom of the ski hill. The figure did not accurately represent the actual number of persons who visited the hill because many visitors failed to register. Twenty-eight towns were represented in the registry, and on the biggest single day, 68 people registered.

The Forest Service considered widening the road to the area and cooperated with the high school ski club to clear the hill. Plans were in the works to build a lodge to replace the temporary shelter. The tentative plans were sent to the Forest Service's regional headquarters in Portland for approval. The lodge was to have a kitchen, front porch, full basement, fireplace and a balcony. World War II put an end to the lodge.

World War II

No discussion of life anywhere in America in the 1940s would be complete without touching on the effect of World War II on the community. As in every town in America, the threat of war and the actual start of war overshadowed nearly everything else in the Methow Valley. The CCC camps and men were swallowed up by the U.S. Army and all local young men registered for the draft.

A 1942 headline in the paper said, "Boys at Head of Winthrop Class Plan to Enter Army" and went on to tell about the boys. Jim Erickson, valedictorian, was student body president and active in skiing and football. In his spare time he managed a ranch and milked 12 cows before and after school. He planned to become a flying cadet.

Howard Brewer was salutatorian, athletic manager, a member of the student council and had received honors in skiing. His plan was to work for the Forest Service during the summer and join the Army in the fall.

Members of the community also supported the war effort. In January 1942, the ladies of Mazama met at the Forest Service warehouse to sew for the Red Cross. They planned to meet again later that month at the home of Mrs. Roy Kumm.

Mr. and Mrs. Rufus Blevins joined thousands of others as air raid spotters who staffed towers up and down the West Coast. The Forest Service moved the Blevins to Slate Peak, where they remained for the duration of the war.

Support groups were formed to help those who remained at home cope with fears about their loved ones at war. For example, a Navy Mothers' Club was organized and met monthly.

Men home on leave were treated with great respect, and buying war bonds was the major promotion of the day. The Sept. 22, 1944, issue of the *Methow Valley News* carried a full-page ad for the First Annual Methow Valley Sportsman Association Dance to be held in the "spacious" Winthrop Auditorium. Tickets were $1. A free war bond was to be given away. The ad said all profit would be used to further "our interests in wildlife and game in the valley."

In 1942, a group of the community's most progressive citizens joined together to help promote the Methow Valley to attract business and tourists. One of their first tasks was to get 28 miles of road built on Harts Pass to connect to the coast. The group included: George Zahn, R.E. Mansfield and Tom Welborn from Pateros, and George Dibble, Jerry Sullivan and W.F. Burge from Winthrop. The group became known as the Methow Valley Chamber of Commerce.

Jack Wilson

Jack Wilson, a master promoter, arrived in the 1940s and purchased HES 84 and 250 on Early Winters Creek. Jack was a self-made man who had been a steel worker on the Golden Gate Bridge and a shipyard worker in Vancouver, Washington. He married a pretty model named Elsie Wheeler and they came to Mazama for a different way of life.

Jack felt there was just about nothing he couldn't do if he put his mind to it, and he set about building cabins for a resort. He built barns and corrals and bought a few horses. Like most men in Mazama, he worked for Hazard Ballard's outfit to learn the packing business. When Hazard's wife Zora eventually had to give up the business after her husband's death, Jack stepped in and gradually purchased harnesses, horses and equipment from her. By 1949, Zora had given Jack her hunting party clients.

Jack Wilson loved packing people into the wilderness.

With Mrs. Ballard's blessings and business referrals, Jack's drive and Elsie's charm, the Wilsons' Early Winters Resort got off to a good start. Jack continued to build cabins and expand his pack string. He did odd jobs on the side to earn money for construction material and furnishings. He bid on trail contracts for the Forest Service and trapped in the winter. Jack was a whirlwind of activity.

He also understood the need to promote his business and the area. He loved the mountains, valley and the wilderness and wanted to share it with all who would listen or come and experience its beauty. He was active in the Sportsman's Council and the Chamber of Commerce and promoted of the North Cross State Highway Association.

Jack was not the most organized businessman but his abilities as a packer and guide were unbeatable. He could take people into the back country, surround them with peace and tranquility and watch them melt into the landscape and become part of nature. Over three decades, Jack became friends with, and had clients who were mayors, governors, congressmen, billionaires, captains of industry and even a Chief Justice of the U.S. Supreme Court (William O. Douglas).

Andy Russell

Andy Russell was another enterprising Mazama resident who did what he could to get by. He farmed, logged and tried his hand at the restaurant business by opening a café and gas pump at Mazama Corners, the junction of Highway 20 and Mazama Road. The most notable thing about the business was its shape – two curved rooms connected by a rectangular structure. It was said to have been built using the forms for a coffer dam on the Columbia River. Andy was a junk collector, so it is quite likely the story is true.

The café was called the Do Drop Inn and it operated off and on, along with a Shell gas pump, for several years during the 1940s. Andy and his wife had it for only about a year before selling it. According to a story in the *Methow Valley News*, it was purchased in 1947 by Mr. and Mrs. Clyde Alexander from Bremerton, Wash.

Napoleon Bowes

Napoleon Bowes was brought into the valley by Andy Russell on one of Andy's trips hauling cattle to the coast. Andy found him walking along the road with rags tied around his feet for shoes. He picked him up. The Russells fed Napoleon and gave him clothes in return for his work.

Napoleon became sort of a community ward, working here and there for food and a place to live. He wasn't sure where he was born (he thought maybe West Virginia), and he didn't know how old he was or who his parents were. It was thought that he was of mixed race because of his dark skin color and features. No one knew if he could read or write. He seemed familiar with just about any place that had a railroad yard, and he spoke of living with Indians, but other than that, the man and his past were a mystery.

Eventually, Napoleon settled into the job of changing sprinklers for Karl Duffy, who owned several places around Little Boulder Creek. Karl fed and clothed him year around and provided firewood. When my family took over Little Boulder Creek Ranch, Napoleon just came with the place and we continued to provide for him as Karl had done.

Napoleon would tell a neighbor what he wanted from the store. The neighbor would call in the order to the grocery store, and the mailman would leave it by the side of the road. Napoleon's bill was charged to the Devin account with no worry that the frugal man would take advantage of the family. Whenever he was given a new shirt or pants, he put them on over his existing clothing and never took the old ones off. He had a stringy black beard and long black hair that he put into an alfalfa sack he used as a hat.

Both Karl and I paid Napoleon in cash. I tried to get him to apply for a Social Security number, but he would have no part of it, saying, "A fellow ought to take care of hisseff." Finally, I got him to agree to having a bank account and he handed over $20 or $30 to deposit. Each bill was tightly rolled like a matchstick. After that, Napoleon's earnings were put in the bank.

Nature seemed to look out for him. He died of a heart attack before the winter of 1968 when the temperature dropped to 50 degrees below zero, which would have been torture for him in his dirt-floored shack. After he died, the sheriff went through his shack and reported finding about $1,800 in small bills hidden in sacks, cans and old socks. The money was used to pay his doctor bills and buy a lot at Sullivan Cemetery.

The Bowers

In 1948, brothers Donald and Harold Bowers, and their parents, Charles and Martha Bowers, bought HES 114, the old Ed Kagle place from Bob and Allan Stookey.

The Bowers had 60 head of Hereford cattle and raised 250 Leghorn chickens. They also built the large block-and-wood barn that is part of the Mazama Ranch House resort today. They sold eggs and chickens (cleaned chickens cost $1). Every fall, they canned hundreds of jars of fruits and vegetables from their garden. Neighbor Guy Sharp always came down to help make sauerkraut.

Charles and Martha Bowers moved to the Mazama area in 1929 from Portland, Oregon. At first they lived in the old store near the Jack Stewart place. Martha cooked for the Mazama Queen Mine crew. Charles hauled logs to the Fender Mill from a piece of land they bought and cleared. They built a house in 1932, almost across the road from the Mt. McKinney School, where Harold attended his first year. He went to school in Winthrop until his junior year, when he dropped out and moved back home to run the farm because his dad had a stroke.

By the time the family bought HES 114, the Mazama Queen was pretty much defunct, so they negotiated with the owners for the cook house building where Martha had once worked and moved it to their land. It was converted into a chicken house. After years of disrepair, the old building, still called the "chicken coop," was renovated in 2004 and became a lounge and meeting room for the Mazama Ranch House resort.

In 1949, Mazama was again in need of a post office. The Bowers stepped off about an acre of land and sold it to Bill and Vi Pederson for $90. The Pedersons opened a store and post office where the Mazama Store sits today.

Looking north up Winthrop's main street, which in this late 1950s photograph shows Shafer's Inc. where today's Emporium stands.

The Flood of 1948

Another major event in the 1940s was the flood of 1948. Many events in the Methow are referred to as having occurred before or after "the '48 flood" and it is mentioned in the recollections of several older residents.

One story recalled by a witness tells of a mishap involving a Winthrop man known for his heavy drinking. After an evening of serious imbibing in Winthrop, the inebriated fellow decided to accompany Knute Pearson to his home in Mazama. It was the first night of the high water, and when the pair got to the Weeman Bridge, they found the approaches were under water. Somehow they made it across.

The next morning, however, the infamous drinker was seen walking down the road in water running knee-deep. The Weeman Bridge was gone, so he headed down Wolf Creek Road to try to get to Winthrop for a drink. The water was running waist-high across the road beyond the Morrow place and the man was washed out into the middle of the river. He grabbed a log that was floating by and made it all the way downstream to the Sunny M Ranch outside Winthrop where, luckily, there was a man on a horse who had been roping. The horseman waded out, threw him a rope and pulled him in.

The flood didn't seem to affect most homes in Mazama, although the community was cut off for several weeks because all the bridges on the Methow River were out.

Zora and Hazard Ballard at their home at Lost River, probably in the 1920s. During his years in the Mazama area Ballard mined in the Slate Creek area, built a portion of the Harts Pass road, and operated a hotel, sawmill and a packing and outfitting business. After his death in 1938, Zora continued the packing business for another 10 years with the help of her brother, Roma Johnson.

Zora Ballard's Diary

After Hazard Ballard died in 1938, his wife Zora continued to run the packing and horse business from their Lost River home on HES 97. Hazard and Zora played major roles in the development of both Rock View and the Robinson/Lost River area. Although they were involved in many enterprises such as building and operating the Rock View Mill, the business venture that lasted the longest for the Ballards was tourism. From the time the Ballards took over the hotel and Last Chance Saloon in Robinson, they were in some form of the tourist business.

Zora kept a diary in her later years, and although the entries mostly describe day-to-day domestic activities, she included two events that became part of Mazama history – the death of a friend, and the flood of '48. The excerpts below are just as Zora wrote them. People mentioned in the diary entries are as follows: Jerry is Edna Farrar, caretaker at Chancellor during the 1940s; Roma Johnson is Zora's brother; Jimmie Sparks is a close friend and sort of an adopted son to Zora; and Sam is probably Sam Bodie, a friend of Hazard Ballard and Jack Wilson from the coast.

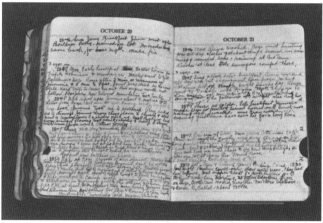

Zora Ballard's diary became an important part of her life after her husband died. She never failed to confide in it, recording the events of the day and what mattered most in her life.

The first event chronicled in Zora's diary begins after Edna "Jerry" Farrar notifies someone, (possibly Jimmie Sparks) that she is leaving from Chancellor. She asks Jimmie to meet her and drive her out. Zora's diaries contain the following entries:

"Oct. 18 (1947), Sat.: Anderson left 9 PM. Sam and friend came 9 PM and went up to meet Jerry, couldn't make it so Jimmie went up with Jeep but saw no one, she was to wait at pass but did not get there. Rained terribly.

"Oct. 19, Sun.: Jimmie, Sam and young man went again to pass in Jeep to look out, walked on 1 mile. 4 hrs snow 3 feet deep worn out came back know nothing of Jerry. Hope she is safe, raining tonight again. Sam left for home. After supper Dents packed out by Roma and Ray 2:30 PM.

"Oct. 20, Mon.: Early Breakfast saddled horses for trip to Robinson and Weeman Cr. Harley went to get Bouldron & Bells. Roma after 2 men on Weeman Cr. Jimmie & 5 men to pass. Found Jerry dead by the road side. Hard trip to carry her out. Poor Angus (the dog) would not follow. Poor Jerry, her beloved mountains took her life.

"Oct. 21, Tues.: Ray went to bring Angus out, he followed, Wright will keep him.

"Oct. 23, Thurs.: Went to Twisp, Anna had a fine dinner ready for us, Lydea there. We all went to church at 2 PM, Jerry had a nice service, flowers beautiful. Dear girl rest in peace."

The October 23, 1947, issue of the *Methow Valley News* carried the story that Zora had chronicled on a daily basis. The headline read: "Edna Coffin Farrar Meets Death on Snowy Harts Pass Trail."

"Found dead by searchers last Monday was Mrs. Edna Coffin Farrar, 60, (who) apparently lost her life in an attempt to pack out from her cabin at the Chancellor Mine, on the west side of Harts Pass.

Mrs. Farrar who has spent the past several years at the cabin during the summer, was to have come out last Saturday, and a party had gone part way up the pass to meet her. Because of the heavy snows and the failure of Mrs. Farrar to appear, the party returned to make preparations to go out after her.

Art Loucks, Clarence Perrine and Chet Knouff of the highway department cleared the way for the searching party Monday morning, and a party of five men from Mazama and Winthrop made their way through three feet of snow, up Harts Pass and at noon they found Mrs. Farrar, her dog beside her, approximately two and a half miles on the west side of Harts Pass.

...She wore no snow shoes and her tracks were found beyond the spot where she was found, indicating that she had started to return to her cabin. Apparently tired from the struggle through the deep snow, Mrs. Farrar was found sitting down on the trail, and it is believed she was a victim of heart failure.

...She spent 15 years working at the United States Mint in Denver... Mrs. Farrar went back to the mine this last spring, continuing her work as a government meteorologist... She thought nothing of carrying a 75 pound pack many miles along the trail."

Another series of entries in Zora's diary described the 1948 flood as she experienced it from her home in Lost River.

"May 24 Mon.: Mr. Green came to phone about Goat Wall Creek washing out road and called Ray (probably Ray Patterson, assistant ranger at the Early Winters station) about trees against Lost River Bridge. State men came and pulled them out, also built bridge over Wall Creek.

"May 25, Tues: Looked at river at 6 AM.

"May 27, Thur.: River high, thunder, power off at 10:30

"May 28, Fri.: Raining, bridge gone, water higher. Hope Mr. Cutler (who lived across Lost River) has plenty of food. Power off but came on at 8 AM for 15 min. Jimmie took Jeep down below Wall Creek. Flooded everywhere. Island all gone by evening. No lights until 10 PM, no news, no mail.

"May 29, Sat.: Water running along hill below grade, all the trees gone on each side of where the bridge was, fill going also, drift formed up stream. Water half way to Cutler's in road. Still raining most of night, no power, no phone. Green came up, Jimmie went down to get dog feed if bridge is still in at Mazama.

"May 30, Sun.: River fell some, lots of drift along sides. Jimmie gone to Wilsons' but Mazama bridge partly gone. 6 bridges out on Methow and many houses washed away at Twisp, no power or phone, food shortage & very little gas. News over battery radio.

"May 31, Mon.: River falling, island forming where bridge was.

"June 1. Tues.: Jimmie and Mr. Green built bridge over Wall Creek.

"June 3, Thur.: Jimmie, Alva & Mr. Green put line across river for Mr. Cutler to get mail.

"June, 9 Wed.: Still no power or phone yet. Listen to prize fight on radio.

"June 10, Thur.: Goat Creek bridged now.

"June 13, Sun.: Wilson visited, went by Weeman Bridge. Rained hard.

"June 24, Thur.: Jimmie worked several days on the bridge, Mr. Cutler crossed tonight with his car."

Zora Ballard died in 1956. Always well regarded, active in the community, wife of a leader and entrepreneur, Zora lived a full life. Her diary reveals, however, that her later years were not among her happiest. She treated Jimmie Sparks as a son and her life revolved around him. She cooked for him and kept house with the expectation that he would act as a son and respond to her kindness. However, he wouldn't show up for meals and vanished for days without telling her. Some felt that he took advantage of Zora, who spent her last years worrying about him.

Folks have been hanging out at the Mazama Store for a long, long time. This photo is from August 1963 and shows, from left, Betsy Devin, Jim Lycett, Cope Miller, Kendall Miller, Downs Miller, and Rick Webber. Steve Devin is standing in the doorway.

Chapter 7

The 1960s
Boosterism and New Projects

The 1960s brought new faces and new projects to the area. Although it was the beginning of another chapter in Mazama history, the boosterism of the 1950s continued into the early 1960s. The ethic of conquering the wilderness lived on, perhaps a little longer in this remote part of the state than in the rest of the West. And the decades-old efforts to build a community and attract new settlers to Mazama continued. Attracting development and industry was a goal as intense as the early settlers' drive to provide public education.

By the end of the 1950s and the beginning of the 1960s, decades of work aimed at bringing the North Cross State Highway to reality was at its height. It was a political matter to get funds for the project, and publicity was an important tool in the political arena. Methow people were good at this and they concocted an event that fit their style and brought attention to their cause. Jack Wilson, an avid highway booster, was one of the chief organizers and provided much of the needed stock and equipment.

Residents staged a Pony Express-style ride over the proposed route for the new highway from Diablo Dam to Early Winters. The *Seattle Times* reported that "Jerry Sullivan, a strong, silent-type cowboy from Winthrop, raced from Diablo Dam, across the Cascade Mountains to Early Winters, exhausting eight horses on a rough, rain-drenched, eight-hour gallop. Fresh mounts were stationed at relay points along the 55-mile up and down route." Summing up the day-long effort, Sullivan said, "Just goes to show why we need this road. If you took available highways you couldn't have made the

Rider Jerry Sullivan finishes an eight-hour ride from Diablo Dam to Early Winters in 1960 and receives congratulations from Les Hollaway, an early booster of the North Cascades highway.

trip as fast by car." An old-fashioned community barbecue capped the day for Mazama and Winthrop supporters.

Getting the North Cross State Highway funded, started and built was still a major community issue, but most of the new settlers in the valley were people looking for an alternative to industry and belching smokestacks. The Puget Sound basin was growing fast and while the Methow was still a six-or-seven-hour trip from Seattle, it was considered by many to be only a few years away from discovery by the masses.

The Mazama store in the late 1960s, when it was run by Bill and Vi Pederson.

Harold and Tina Heath

Harold Heath was a self-made man and an industrialist in the true sense of the word. Based in Seattle, he built an empire that got its start serving the aircraft industry. Heath Techna manufactured interiors for commercial aircraft. The firm expanded into diversified industries and the company's stock was actively traded publicly. Harold was a wealthy business tycoon with all the advantages and disadvantages that accompany such a position in society.

A negative aspect of Harold's position was stress, and the need to escape from the constant pressures of business. To this end, Harold frequented the finest resorts, spas and retreats only to find that instead of relaxing, he was in a social whirl, getting dressed up, meeting people and staying up late. He had to find a spot to really get away. On a business trip to the Okanogan he asked an associate if he knew of a place that was like the Okanogan but with trees. His friend suggested the Methow Valley. On this suggestion, Harold met real estate agents Lewis Cooley and Grace Walsh.

Harold purchased the Golden Doe Ranch between Twisp and Carlton in 1963 and the Big Buck Ranch up the Twisp River in 1965. He bought 1,500 acres on the valley bottom near the inter-city airport southeast of Winthrop in 1966. The next year, he bought 1,200 acres in Rock View from the McCauley family. The property consisted of the Albert Ventzke place, the original H.H. Johnson homestead, some of the Wehmeyer homesteads and other land that had been assembled by the Cooper family.

The same year, Harold bought the 160-acre Boesel place, and the following year he purchased 220 acres from the Holcombs and a large piece by the river from Gamble Lumber Co. Finally, in 1972 Harold bought the last 120-acre piece and completed what he called the Big Valley Ranch. In addition, Harold was buying up orchards along with Lewis Cooley, who owned the bank in Twisp.

Harold and Tina Heath in 2007 with the Big Valley Ranch in the background.

Jim McCauley, a local man who was part of the former owner's family, managed the Big Valley Ranch. McCauley hired Walt Holcomb as his assistant and together they ran a cattle operation of fairly big scale by Methow Valley standards. They had lots of hay and pasture land, plenty of range and the money to buy good machines and equipment.

Two significant events brought Harold's buying spree to a halt. First, Mother Nature produced the winter of 1967-68 with record low valley temperatures of 50 degrees below zero. That season the orchard segment of his business suffered a $750,000 loss. Next, a recession tumbled the price of Heath Techna stock from $120 to $7 a share and finally to a low of $1 a share. Harold was forced to liquidate his holdings to cover the loans he had taken to acquire them. One by one he sold them off at bargain prices. He combined operations and cut expenses as best he could. As if this weren't enough bad luck, at about the same time the Heath's home in south Seattle burned to the ground.

When Heath Techna was in its prime, Harold had supported a young man who left Boeing to start his own fiberglass business by helping him obtain financing and giving him work Heath Techna didn't want to do. The man became quite successful manufacturing fiberglass panels for trucks. When Harold found himself out of a job after his own company got into trouble, the man he had once helped gave him a job. By then the company had moved to Ohio to be closer to the truck manufacturing business.

Harold and his wife Tina left the area in1976 and went to Cincinnati, Ohio, to start over. Harold took charge of sales and helped build the business from a share value of $2 to $32, then sold out and returned to his Big Valley Ranch. (Art Davis looked after the ranch while they were gone and Aaron Burkhart leased it until 1982.) Once back in the valley, the Heaths dove into the community. Tina was elected to the school board and was part of the Mazama Advisory Committee working on a community master plan.

Harold, who had always dreamed of being in the cow business, jumped in with 500 head his first year and later had as many as 900 head. But raising cattle wasn't as profitable as he planned, so he started leasing his fields to other ranchers for so much per cow/ calf pair. That arrangement did work out and he continued to do so into the 1990s.

In 1991, the Washington Wildlife and Recreation Coalition successfully lobbied the state legislature for money to buy part of the ranch on the valley floor on the condition that the Heaths could remain on the ranch and graze cattle. The coalition wanted to preserve the land as pasture and open space and prevent its development. Since 1991, Harold has pastured cattle on the ranch under a renewable five-year lease agreement with the coalition. As long as Harold continues to use the land as pasture, the coalition will continue to renew the lease.

The coalition's purchase was a wonderful gift to the valley and those who love it. Today hundreds of residents and visitors use the nature, bike, horse and ski trails on the Big Valley Ranch. However, as with any decision of significant impact, there were those who at the time questioned the propriety of spending public funds in this manner. Nonetheless, the purchase ensured preservation of vistas and open fields that are considered a "signature view" of the upper Methow Valley.

Jack and Elsie Wilson's Early Winters Resort

Development of the Early Winters Resort began to hit its stride in the mid-1960s. Jack Wilson stopped adding buildings. Elsie ran the business. She cleaned the cabins, did the laundry in the wash house, kept the accounts, handled reservations and supervised a wrangler who helped with the horses and rides. Jack did maintenance, managed marketing and did the dreaming.

Things weren't all rosy, though. Jack had been contracting to do trail work and had lost a bundle of money. He had a way of thinking a job was easier than it actually turned out to be and under-bid on some big sections of trail construction. He was in debt and the bank was calling the loan.

Jack was making some money packing for hunters and fishermen and working his wilderness trip business. Elsie's work at the cabins made it a profitable business but not profitable enough to pay off the debt from her husband's trail-building fiasco. Fortunately, Jack was saved because he was able to borrow money from an old friend to stave off foreclosure. (That friend was Kay Wagner, widow of Otto Wagner, who had owned Wagner Lumber Company in Twisp. Kay later spearheaded Winthrop's westernization.)

Young guests at the Early Winters Resort ride along a dirt road that today is part of Highway 20.

However, money problems didn't seem to bother Jack very much. He once bought a horse knowing he would be in trouble with Elsie. So he named the horse "Hay" and gave Elsie the bill to pay as an expense.

Elsie would worry and fret, but Jack went on dreaming about bigger and better things – building the North Cross State Highway, promoting the Methow, managing the wilderness area and operating the Washington State Department of Fish and Game. The department was one of his pet peeves. While his objectives were nearly the same as the agency's – the enhancement of wildlife – he felt the state bureaucrats didn't have a clue about game management and said so in no uncertain terms.

Jack and Elsie Wilson raised this orphaned fawn after its mother was killed on the highway.

About this time, Jack began to figure out how to make some money during the winter. His business was strictly a summer and fall operation. During the first few winters he spent in Mazama, he trapped. He would snowshoe miles up Early Winters Creek and stay in a small log shelter (located where Lone Fir Campground is today) and trap the creeks that flow into Early Winters. Eventually, when the price for hides dropped but the difficulty of trapping remained the same, Jack pondered the possibility of winterizing his cabins and catering to skiers.

There was a nice little hill behind the cabins. In addition to skiing, Jack could offer sleigh rides and people could snowshoe around the fields and up the trails along Early Winters Creek. (At the time, cross-country skiing in this area was virtually nonexistent except as a competitive sport.) Jack shared his idea with me as a longtime friend and summer guest of the resort.

I was in the ski business. I had been active in the establishment of Crystal Mountain and was a supervisor at the ski school there. And I was also in the ski equipment part of the industry as a retailer, wholesaler and manufacturer. I was aware of the need for more ski facilities in the state if the sport was to continue to grow, and what would be necessary for a successful ski resort. The hill behind the cabins where Jack was considering putting a simple lift, had only a few hundred feet of vertical drop and would not justify anything more than a beginner hill. When I told Jack that it probably would not work, we got out maps and began looking at other possibilities. We found that around the corner there was a north-facing hill called Sandy Butte with 4,000 feet of drop and variable terrain. This appeared to be too good to be true.

Jack arranged for an inspection trip that fall. I was more than a little impressed with what we discovered and set about gathering more information, such as snow depths, temperatures, weather conditions, snow characteristics and the availability of private property at the base of the hill. This last factor, the availability of private property, was essential. I shared my findings and opinions with several colleagues in the ski industry and all concurred that if a feasibility study could be completed with favorable results, a first-class ski area in Washington state could become a reality.

Skiers and industry people had always recognized that a high-quality ski area would need to be on the east slope of the Cascades to get the weather and snow quality that people traveled to the Rocky Mountains to find. They also knew that private property was necessary to help finance a resort with accommodations and year-round activities.

I enlisted the support and enthusiasm of neighbor Len Miller, who owned HES 89 and 90, property that would be critical to any development. Len was an active skier, avalanche consultant and photographer, skills useful in completion of the feasibility study. It was a totally volunteer effort. Len and I formed the Methow Valley Winter Sports Council, comprised of Methow Valley community leaders and experienced ski industry people.

Dr. Bill Henry and his wife Ann were skiers and active in the community. Bill was chairman of the council. Lew Cooley, a Twisp banker, was treasurer and undertook the task of raising money to help cover expenses. Ski industry notables on the council included Jack Nagel, a former Olympian and head of the Crystal Mountain Ski School; Mike Ewing, a professional ski patrolman from Vail; and Bob Cram, a writer, illustrator and host of a weekly television ski show in Seattle.

This group, along with others, made a major assault on the mountain equipped with cameras, altimeters, slope-meters and measuring devices. It was the first major effort to obtain good information and expert opinions. Len Miller already had made a couple of trips to the summit, although not with the feasibility study in mind. He found the best route up and good ski runs down.

This flurry of activity occurred in March 1968, a winter of record low temperatures and superb snow conditions. In January, Mazama recorded a temperature of 52 degrees below zero, the lowest ever recorded in Washington state. As the skiers cruised down

This trapper's cabin was moved from Lone Fir Campground to the Early Winters Ranger Station in the early 1970s when Highway 20 was built. Jack Wilson was one of numerous men who had used it for mid-winter shelter during their years of trapping.

through meadows and clear-cuts, cameras filmed powder snow flying shoulder-high behind them and the rooster tail of snow evaporating almost entirely before it fell back to the ground. It was some of the best skiing these world-traveled ski professionals had ever seen. The films were incorporated into a televison show by Bob Cram and later made into a movie that was shown far and wide that showed the butte's ski potential.

Buying Land at Early Winters.

I completed the feasibility study the next year but even before it was finished, skiers and industry people were hearing about Early Winters in the Methow. This posed a serious problem. If the group was to attract a major firm or developer, it would be next to impossible to gather all the necessary land at a reasonable cost if there were great speculation in land values.

It was also at this time that the Shafers approached me, as a friend, and asked if I was interested in buying their land. A developer had been working with Dorothy Shafer to purchase and subdivide their place, but he had made Dorothy mad in the process. By then the Shafers had purchased property in the Columbia Basin and wanted to move there. I said I would see what I could do.

When the idea of developing a ski area at Sandy Butte emerged, Jack Wilson, Doug Devin and Claude Miller, left to right, were among the volunteers who made snowshoe and snow cat trips into the mountains near Early Winters to record terrain, snow and weather observations.

A group of people with money was needed to buy the land and "bank" it so a resort developer would not have to outbid speculators for pieces necessary for the project. Finding people with money to invest in land who were willing to take a large risk and then turn the land over without maximizing their profit was not easy. They had to be people who saw the development of great skiing as equal to, or more important than, profiting from a good investment.

I found such individuals among my associates in the ski industry and at Crystal Mountain – directors and the chairman of Crystal Mountain, the former owners of A&T Ski Co., (a large national pioneering ski manufacturer based in Seattle) and a group of ski instructors. This group purchased the Shafer ranch, HES 91, 92 and 93, and then over time purchased the land owned by Len and Dianne Miller, HES 89 and 90.

A half-dozen smaller parcels of from one to five acres proved difficult to purchase because each owner thought he was in a powerful position and could get a big price by being a holdout. In addition, the Millers were starting to market a 36-lot subdivision, which had to be stopped and the owners satisfied. I worked on the difficult and time-consuming task of land purchase for several years.

By the end of 1969, the Winter Sports Council had met with Forest Service officials and told them of the group's activities. Forest Service officials indicated they also had been aware of Sandy Butte's potential for skiing and had it on a list to be considered in future studies.

Edelweiss

While planning was going on for an Early Winters ski resort, a large second-home development called Edelweiss was underway across the valley on the hillside up river from the Weeman Bridge. The owners were advertising hundreds of lots from one-half to two acres in size complete with water and underground power. Camping areas by the river and plans for a community swimming pool also were drawing cards.

Bill Laney, a Seattle insurance executive, and Norm Hamilton, an orchardist, had fallen in love with the valley and put together partners to purchase the land from Aaron Burkhart. It was the largest and most ambitious project of this type ever tried in the upper valley. Bill and his partner planned to create a development that would be environmentally sensitive but still profitable. Bill got into the deal in 1963 because he just wanted a place to build a summer cabin. He called George Dibble, a banker in Winthrop, who suggested he talk to Burkhart, who might have land for sale. Bill ended up buying 550 acres for $120,000 ($220 an acre) and found himself in the land development business.

Bill and Norm hired Don Drake as general manager and started on the first of four plats that eventually would be developed under a set of covenants and restrictions patterned after Seattle's Windermere district. The first plat consisted of lots on the river and camp sites in the flood plain that sold for $2,400 with 10 percent down. The second plat consisted of 80 lots of one or two acres on the benches above the river. The developers committed to installing a water and underground power system. But the lots did not sell well.

The project was costing big money and the partners were scrambling to obtain financing. Sales were not enough to cover cash-flow requirements. For two years in the early 1970s, the county road on that side of the river, Goat Creek Road, was closed for reconstruction. Sales were disastrously few. In addition to the road problem, Seattle's economy was doing poorly. The partners were $200,000 in debt and Norm Hamilton was unable to put any more money into the project.

Bill sold his business to cover part of the debt, but with no sales and no market, the project was still headed for bankruptcy. Through his family Bill was able to borrow enough to keep going, but he still had to sell some lots. He went to The Johns Co., a firm of former servicemen operating out of Okinawa that sold investments to servicemen on a payroll deduction plan. It seemed to be a good combination. Bill liked the firm, and its salesmen were excited about the project after a visit to the site.

It worked. The entire inventory of lots sold within 12 months. The sales company received every penny of the 20 percent down payments and Bill got the contracts.

It was now the mid-1970s and with the North Cascades Highway open and increasing excitement about the potential ski area at Sandy Butte, the sales solved the cash-flow problem. Within a few years, Edelweiss lots were being resold by the original buyers and nearly all made a nice profit on their investment. But it would be a number of years before Bill and his partners got their money back and even longer before they made a modest profit.

Originally there were 360 lots in Edelweiss, although over the years some have been combined. By fall 2007 there were houses on about half the properties – three-quarters of them owned by part-time residents.

A spring 1960s view of Mazama from Sandy Butte with snow still visible on Goat Peak – a signal to locals that it is still too early to plant their gardens.

Early Winters Resort opened three cabins for winter use in the 1970s to attract cross-country skiers.

Chapter 8

The 1970s
The Highway Opens,
New People Arrive,
The Ski Resort Battle Erupts

The most significant events in the history of Mazama and the upper Methow Valley were the discovery of gold in the Slate Creek area in the 1890s and the opening of the North Cascades Highway in 1972. Both brought scores of people into the valley, many of them to make a new life here. Of course, the highway was not a surprise. It was under discussion for about 70 years and under construction for five.

Real estate sales in the Mazama area flourished as talk of road construction began, and the pace only intensified during and after construction. Subdivisions of every size were marketed mostly by amateur speculators, although some land was divided and sold by older residents who had waited a lifetime to get a decent price for their land.

Many one-acre lots were put on the market without much success. The owners of one development called Bonanza Acres, on Lost River Road at HES 197, divided acres of flood plain and attempted to sell lots when the land was dry in late summer. Some lots were only 100 feet wide, but they were 900 feet long and stretched from the road to the river, so they could be sold as two-acre, river-front lots.

Generally, it was too early to sell lots. The only buyers were speculators, a few hunters and some people who dreamed of eventually moving to the valley. But few who discovered the beautiful upper Methow could afford to live or retire here without an outside income. Some people chose to live in Mazama and work in Winthrop or Twisp; others left the valley for a few months at a time to earn money and then returned.

By the 1970s, local industry was gone. There were no jobs in mining, logging had wound down and the sawmill in Twisp had ceased operation. With a few exceptions, viable agriculture no longer existed. The U.S. Forest Service was the largest employer, although most work was seasonal. But the new highway brought the opportunity to develop the tourist and recreation industries. Not everyone liked the reality, but the Methow Valley was now accessible and open to the world. Thousands of travelers started passing over the spectacular North Cascades Highway on a drive destined to become one of the state's major tourist attractions.

Lifestyle Changes

Like scores of other rural towns and small Western communities throughout the country, the Methow Valley experienced what the old-time locals called a "hippie infestation" in the 1960s and 1970s. Here, the so-called "hippies" mostly came from Western Washington and California, although young folks arrived from almost everywhere, including New York and other East Coast locales. They moved into what seemed to be every house, shack and cave in the area. Most meant well and planned to "live off the land," a popular lifestyle at the time portrayed in movies, nature books and magazines.

One group lived in the house on HES 95 by Gate Creek until it burned down. Another moved into the Welch house on HES 91 with the plan of fixing it up and working for Don Shafer. They started by taking out the windows and doors and taking down part of the chimney. But when the weather got cold, the group, which hailed from southern California, vanished and the house never recovered. The cold Mazama winters forced most of the young newcomers, especially those without real houses, out of the valley or down to Twisp.

Even after the exodus, the new winter "hippie" population nearly equaled the locals. They entered into local activities such as the community potluck dinners and card parties with great gusto but their appetites often exceeded their contributions. Moreover, their contributions usually consisted of foods like tofu or organic apples, not always appreciated by the palettes of old-time Mazama people. Despite differences in lifestyle, these new folks added spice to life in Mazama and were an important connection to the outside world.

The Mazama Bible Camp

During the summer of 1970, Jess and Francis Hintz, a farm couple from Ohio, visited the Methow on their way to Arizona with a load of blankets and clothing for the Hopi Indians. The couple visited the Mazama Community Church, where they talked about their trip and their interest in mission work. A few months later they received a phone call asking whether they would be interested in being temporary pastors of the church and caretakers of the nearby Mazama Bible Camp.

Jess and Francis put their farm up for sale on a Monday in January 1971. It sold on Tuesday, reaffirming their decision. They loaded a U-Haul trailer, packed the family in a couple of cars – three girls, two of them married, and two boys. The party of nine arrived at midnight on February 1, 1971, and were here to stay.

Nobody seems to know how or when the Bible camp land was transferred from the original

The Mazama Community Church congregation started meeting in the 1950s, although this church building wasn't constructed until the 1980s.

homesteader to the group of U.S. and Canadian citizens who established the camp. Recollections are that it was first used in the 1930s as a camp site with fire pit. In about 1948, the owners group built rustic camping structures that were offered to Christian church groups for summer camping and Bible study.

The Mazama Community Church was started in the 1950s as an outgrowth of Sunday school meetings previously held at various locations. In 1952, Dr. John Malzacher, who owned HES 202, (the Devin Ranch today), donated a house that sat north of Little Boulder Creek. It was moved a few hundred yards down the road and became the church. At some point the church and camp joined forces to obtain a pastor and camp caretaker. Wesley Mansfield did the mostly volunteer job for awhile, but eventually left the valley.

In the early 1980s, construction of the new State Highway 20 took out most of the church property and all the parking space. Officials of the Bible camp and the church, which was pretty much on its own by then, agreed that the church could build on camp property. Jess Hintz oversaw most of the construction. He retired in 1996 after 27 years as a "temporary" pastor of the Mazama Community Church and 25 years as director of the Mazama Bible Camp.

After Jess retired, there were several pastors. Volunteers led by Clyde Allen finished the new log church building. The congregation applied for support from Village Missions, an organization that supports pastors in rural U.S. and Canadian communities.

About the same time, Randy Picklesimer, a building contractor from the Everett area, decided to become a full-time pastor and part-time builder. Village Missions decided to support the Mazama church and offered Randy the assignment. He moved to the Methow Valley with his wife Lisa and their three high-school-age children in 2001. Randy remodeled the Bible camp house and helped Clyde finish the church. Today the camp is run by a seven-person board.

Ski Industry Growth

The ski industry experienced tremendous growth both in equipment development and resorts during the 1970s. Equipment that made skiing both easier and safer brought tens of thousands of new skiers to the sport every year. It became the "in" sport both in Europe and North America. Fashion and dining were important related elements. Thus the concept of skiing broadened from a sport to a lifestyle. Skiing became an industry and major economic generator.

Towns and entire provinces in Austria grew and flourished because of their locations in the mountains and the quality of the skiing and hospitality offered. Virtual ghost towns in Colorado sprang to life if skiing were available. Old miners and ranchers on the verge of bankruptcy struck sudden wealth.

Many individuals, as well as the state and several local governments, in Washington wanted to share this prosperity. Oddly, most backers of skiing in the Methow, including founders of the Methow Winter Sports Council, were not motivated to "get rich," nor were they in a position to benefit much financially. They were people who loved the sport and simply wanted a good place to ski closer to home than Colorado or Idaho. While a number of them bought real estate, it was to build a house for themselves, not to engage in speculative investment. They were sportsmen and dreamers, not hard-nosed businessmen and developers. So when these people went looking for funds and experienced individuals to build a major resort, they really didn't know where to turn or what to do.

My main tool for selling development of a ski resort in the upper Methow was a 20-minute film containing scenes of skiing through glorious powder snow that had been shown on Bob Cram's Seattle television show, combined with footage of potential summer activities filmed by Jeff Pritchard, a cinematography student at the University of Southern California.

I purchased a second-hand movie projector and lugged it around along with the film and copies of the feasibility study. I talked to anyone who would listen. Sports council members and ski industry people suggested persons to speak with and arranged interviews. I talked with Boise Cascade, a forest products company that was into recreational real estate. I talked with a representative of the Teamsters Union Pension Fund who was looking for long-term investments.

Aspen Arrives

One of the great ski development success stories in the early 1970s was Vail, Colorado. Flush with success, Vail managers were looking to expand. Mike Ewing, a former ski industry employee in Colorado who later moved to Seattle, and Bob Parker, the Vail marketing manager and a personal friend, talked Vail management into taking a look at Early Winters. Vail President Pete Seibert and some of his staff made the trip to enjoy fishing in the Methow but also to see what else the area had to offer.

Like Vail, the Aspen Skiing Corporation was looking for new ventures. Aspen was the older, larger firm and was considerably more structured in its expansion efforts. It assigned the task of finding ways to expand to its planning department, which started actively looking for development opportunities from a list of nearly 300 possible sites.

Early Winters came to its attention because it was on the Forest Service list of potential ski-area sites. Jerry Blann of Aspen contacted me for more information. The area looked good on paper, so Aspen President Darcy Brown and Blann made several visits. They hired a helicopter and flew up, down and around the mountain and base area and decided it was one of the best prospects they had seen to date.

Brown, a former Colorado state legislator, also had been a cattle rancher in Colorado and Utah. He was a "country boy" at heart and had a feel for the rural values held by valley residents. He was honest

Jerry Blann, a planner for the Aspen Skiing Corporation, worked on the local ski resort plan for a time. Here he speaks at a community meeting in 1975.

and open, called things as he saw them and was liked by all who came in contact with him. Blann was 29 at the time and part of Aspen's planning department. He had grown up in the ski business. His father was the ski area manager at Mt. Bachelor in Bend, Oregon, and Blann had been a ski racer of note. Later in his career, he would plan the Blackcomb Resort in Whistler, B.C., and become president of Aspen Skiing Company. Today Blann is president and chief operating officer of a company that runs a ski resort in Jackson, Wyoming.

The Aspen company had a relatively active and prestigious board of directors, including former Secretary of Defense Robert McNamara, former Secretary of the Navy and U.S. chief United Nations arms negotiator Paul Nitze, Coors Brewing Company owner Bill Coors, as well as other prominent and affluent persons.

After Brown and Blann made their preliminary report, Aspen's board approved pursuing the Early Winters site and obtaining options on real estate to allow base development. Blann was assigned to the project full time and moved his family to the little house that Len Miller had built on HES 89.

Blann charged into the tasks of completing a detailed feasability study and a preliminary design for the mountain. He hired scores of consultants and embarked on a state-of-the-art technical and environmental assessment of the area. This was 1975 and environmental planning was a relatively new concept, especially for communities like the Methow. Tens of thousands of dollars were spent on studies of local water, air, transportation, geology, soils and archaeology.

Blann encouraged Okanogan County officials to expedite planning and paid for Joe Porter, a planning specialist from Colorado, to assist. Acting as chairman of the Citizens Land Use Advisory Committee, I held dozens of public meetings to get community participation in a draft comprehensive plan and zoning ordinance to prepare the community and the county for growth and to prevent strip development by speculators. Public education was an important factor in getting a zoning ordinance adopted. Many parts of the county were very conservative and a great many citizens felt zoning was a forerunner of Communism.

The investor group I formed was able to offer the critical 400 acres at the base of Sandy Butte and it helped Aspen obtain options on other parcels. The Cassal Ranch had been purchased by a group led by Lew Cooley, so that large piece was included. Darcy Brown put together a deal for Jack and Elsie Wilson that allowed them to pay off their debt to Mrs. Wagner, receive a sizeable payment and stay on 10 acres of their place rent-free in a house Jack would build with a $20,000 contribution from Aspen. Brown also made a deal to purchase the house and land from Ellis and Martha Peters that gave them cash and the right to continue living rent-free in their house for the rest of their lives.

When Aspen's actions and efforts became public knowledge, the result was the first "land rush" in the upper valley since the area was opened to homesteading. The majority of buyers were from Aspen, Colorado – people who had witnessed firsthand the demand for real estate near a ski resort.

Aspen Opponents

At the same time real estate speculators were showing an interest, a "counter-culture" group was moving into the valley, along with people who called themselves "urban refugees." Some of the latter also were from Aspen but others came from California, Connecticut and everywhere in between. Some newcomers joined the Twisp Grange, a symbol to them of rural and agricultural life. Some tried their hand at logging. A few obtained seasonal work with the Forest Service. Nearly all were well educated, not only with college degrees but wise in ways of "working the system." Some were experienced grant writers and they put their skill to work. They managed to get grants for all kinds of projects – from building hot houses to interviewing migrant workers.

Maggie Coon was one of the urban refugees, a young woman who came to the valley in 1975 to assist a former professor preparing a planning report for the Forest Service. When the report was done, she stayed. Her mission, as described in an extensive article in the *Seattle Weekly* newspaper, was to "defeat the Aspen Skiing corporation's plans for a resort." The article described Maggie as "young, college-educated and a daughter of Eastern privilege ... She is clear eyed and articulate, a natural leader of her peers."

The story went on to explain, "Although Maggie does, in fact, earn what money she needs to support herself, her 26-acre spread on the banks of the river was bought with money from her family, and that alone is enough to make some of the hard-bitten ranchers fiercely resentful."

Regardless of the feelings of the old-timers, the counter-culture newcomers were established in the valley in numbers. The group had strength and influenced organizations such as the Grange. A few older citizens supported their position. Grants were obtained for projects such as "grassroots publications" to fight growth.

In spring of 1975, according to the *Weekly* article, Coon decided that more cohesive opposition was needed. She made a trip to Seattle to solicit help from environmental groups. This resulted in a visit from a representative of the Wilderness Society, who assisted Coon and others in organizing the Methow Valley Citizens Council.

The most acute concerns of resort opponents were the social and economic impacts on the valley. Land prices in the upper valley rose as news of Aspen's plan spread and Coon warned that prices would continue to skyrocket as the development took shape. She said that she felt that for ranchers in the northern part of the valley, the pressure to develop land for recreational homes would be enormous. Despite the decline of agriculture in the valley, many people felt it was worth taking positive steps to preserve land for rural uses rather than convert it to recreational use. And ski culture was eyed with great suspicion by those opposed to Aspen. The MVCC made much of alpine skiers' alleged reputation for sex and drug use.

Proponents did not equate what had happened in Colorado with the plans they had for the Methow. Twisp banker and realtor Lew Cooley said that the opponents of growth did "more to upset our lifestyle than anything else possibly could."

"Anti-hippie" sentiment reached new heights as a result of the Aspen plan. One of the Aunt Hattie columns that ran in the *Methow Valley News* as part of the Abrams Chevrolet ad said: "Tell all of your Seattle hunters, if they don't get stampeded by a deer, not to go home empty handed, take a hippie. They are kind of hard to clean, but with an apple in their mouth they make good decorations on the fender of the car."

Mining Interests Return

There also was renewed interest in mining in the mid-1970s, which sparked additional environmental issues. This resurgence was not coming from the old prospectors of the gold rush days and did not involve the stock-selling schemes of the first half of the 1900s. Rather, this was a sophisticated and well-funded operation. The Quintana Mining Company had claims on Flag Mountain, located on the northeast side of Mazama facing Sandy Butte, the site of the proposed ski resort.

Quintana did not operate as openly as Aspen. It quietly went about the business of drilling core samples to analyze ore and stake more claims. Quintana planned to develop an open pit mine one mile long, one-half mile wide and 1,500 feet deep when copper reached $1 a pound, which the company estimated would be within five years. Because the ore reportedly was low grade, the rock was to be washed with massive amounts of water. Opponents believed the mine would create more severe water quality problems than any ski resort. The mining issue got the attention of environmentalists and nearly everyone in Mazama.

To further complicate things, Vernon LaMotte, a mining engineer and geologist from a pioneer valley family who was a member of the MVCC, supported plans for a mine. Asked why a mine would be acceptable but not a ski area, his response was, "They're our kind of people."

Suddenly ski area supporters were battling the anti-development MVCC and fighting Quintana on environmental grounds. They felt that the environmental damage created by the mine would be drastically damaging to a resort atmosphere that would attract tourists to the valley as a whole. They were frustrated because the MVCC appeared to take no stand on the mine. Even some of the new anti-growth counter-culture people felt mining was more in keeping with the rural nature of the valley.

By 1974 Blann and the Aspen company had become a very visible part of the community and had hired a helper for the task of completing the feasibility study and preliminary layout of the mountain. He was Tucker Barksdale, a young man who had degrees in forestry and geology. He was the son of well-known University of Washington geology professor Julian Barksdale, who had spent a lifetime studying and writing about the geology of the Methow Valley.

By 1975 state-of-the-art technicians were in high gear planning for a major resort. A second feasibility study was completed for the Aspen directors. While all aspects of the resort looked promising from a business point of view, the permitting process looked difficult for the foreseeable future.

The top third of the mountain was in a roadless area even though the bottom portion had been logged out. The roadless land theoretically was a candidate for wilderness designation regardless of its other qualifications or circumstances. Hence no action was possible for the land until completion of a study called RARE I, a later study called RARE II, and eventually, the passage of the Washington Wilderness Bill in Congress.

Sun Mountain and Cross-Country Skiing

The mid-1970s also saw the development of cross-country skiing at Sun Mountain Lodge, which had been built primarily as a summer resort and an extension of the old Sunny M Dude Ranch. Owner and developer Jack Baron closed the resort in winter but had to hire one or two people to maintain the facility, keep it heated and plow the road – fixed costs with zero income.

The first sanctioned cross-country ski race in the Methow Valley was sponsored by the Early Winters Ski Club with help from the U.S. Ski Association in the early 1970s. The race attracted skiers from throughout the state and introduced them to local snow.

Dave Chantler, who worked at Recreational Equipment, Inc., in Seattle, proposed in the early '70s that Jack generate income by opening the lodge for groups of cross-country skiers sponsored by REI, which is now a national mountaineering and outdoor gear cooperative. The idea made sense.

The first winter season was short. Jack hired Terry Haynes to be a "one-man show." Haynes was director of recreational activities at the resort, played guitar, sang and organized activities. He rented skis, laid out trails and did some trail grooming. However, he was more interested in alpine skiing than cross-country and eventually relocated to Aspen.

About this time, my family and friends laid out and cleared cross-country ski trails on the Aspen property. Jack Wilson kept three of his cabins open in winter, and I had pamphlets printed describing cross-country skiing in the valley.

Don and Sally Portman came to Sun Mountain in 1976 and opened a cross-country ski shop. Don was instrumental in forming what would become the Methow Valley Ski Touring Association (MVSTA), the entity that started laying out and grooming trails in the upper valley. Don continues to be director of skiing at Sun Mountain. The groomed ski trails, scenic vistas, gentle terrain and sunshine were central to the growing reputation of Methow Valley skiing.

At first there were many separate efforts to maintain trails with snowmobiles. Don had the most extensive trail system at Sun Mountain. Jack Wilson was grooming in Mazama on the Aspen property. Trails were started at Rendevous Mountain that eventually developed into an extensive hut-to-hut experience. Dick Hamel, a Winthrop motel operator, developed trails around town. In all, there were more than 50 miles of trails, which made the Methow Valley noteworthy nationwide.

In 1978, a Mazama ski group sponsored the first local cross-country ski race to be officially sanctioned by the Pacific Northwest Ski Association. It was called the Early Winters Nordic Classic. This event introduced many competitive skiers to the area for the first time. Jack Wilson was there in his cowboys boots, as was Claude Miller with a sleigh and team of horses. Bess Karro was among the Mazama women who baked goodies for the participants. However, Nordic skiing continued to grow slowly in Mazama because attention was focused on building a hill for alpine skiing.

Aspen Departs

The provincial government of British Columbia had been wooing Aspen to develop ski facilities at Blackcomb Mountain adjacent to Whistler Mountain. It was too good a deal to refuse. Aspen left the Mazama project and moved to Canada. The company predicted that it could develop in Canada then return to restart the Mazama project when the wilderness issues were resolved. The Canadian project went well. But before it was complete the Aspen Skiing Company was purchased by Twentieth Century Fox and the Aspen people and all their businesses were caught up in the world of buy-out/spin-off mergers.

The Early Winters project was a relatively small item in the universe of huge resorts and movies and thus went generally unnoticed by Fox for some time. Blann had been promoted to senior management and when the option period on the real estate was up, he was able to convince the real estate division at Fox that it was a good investment. Fox purchased the property but soon spun it off to Urban Aetna, a group involved in constructing high-rise office buildings in large cities. It became evident that the new owners were not interested in building a ski resort in Washington state.

Thus, together with people from the Methow and the Seattle people who had assembled the land Aspen purchased, I formed a company called Methow Recreation Inc. and proceeded to apply for a Forest Service permit to build a ski area.

Part of the option agreement with Aspen stated that if it did not develop, it would turn over to the sellers (myself and friends) all the studies and engineering data it had assembled. Aspen complied with this agreement and these studies, worth a quarter of a million dollars, were the principal capital that launched MRI.

The MRI directors were a cross-section of interest groups. I was president and managing director. The other directors were Scott Detro, a retailer from Riverside (near Omak); Walt Hampton, general manager of Mission Ridge ski area; David Gossard, an attorney from Seattle; Claude Miller, a packer/outfitter from Winthrop; and Bob Ulrich, a Twisp pharmacist. In 1978, using the studies and engineering that had been developed by Aspen, MRI officially submitted an application for a permit and supplied the data necessary for the Forest Service to start the process and write the required Environmental Impact Statement. It was a large task and the most complex evaluation Okanogan National Forest ever had undertaken.

Throughout the 1970s the Methow Valley community was taking dramatic steps towards acceptance of a new comprehensive plan and zoning ordinance, a radical undertaking at the time for a rural county. Dozens of meetings were held on land use, and members of the Methow Valley Citizens Council, which opposed the ski area and growth in the Methow, took an active role in all the meetings and public hearings. They were articulate, well-prepared and usually garnered support from the audience.

Many locals and old-timers felt overwhelmed by the organization and apparent power of these "no-growthers." The business community and much of the upper valley "establishment," including Jack Abrams, a former county commissioner, set up an organization called Citizens for Planned Growth, CPG. It received contributions from the community and local businesses and hired as executive secretary, Edison "Pete" Arnold, a retired U.S. Air Force pilot and officer who had built a private air strip at Lost River and subdivided the area into hundreds of lots.

Arnold's development offered purchasers the opportunity to fly their planes to a remote and beautiful place and park them in front of their own private cabins. He was a developer and proud of it. He felt that proper development and recreation offered the only economic opportunities for the valley and he wanted to stop the "no growth" newcomers from preventing existing landowners from exploiting their opportunities. He was a moderate who favored zoning and controls on growth but didn't want to see the valley closed to development.

CPG appeared to be relatively successful. It signed up many members, collected enough money to keep the organization running and had a significant influence on the outcome of zoning issues. After this success, Arnold decided to run for county commissioner. His race was against Archie Eiffert, a local man who had been mayor of Twisp. They were both Republicans and had similar political views. Arnold lost the primary to Eiffert, who had long-time support and name recognition, then devoted himself to helping Archie win the seat in the general election.

A great many issues put forward by the Methow Valley Citizens Council proved to be important for the valley if growth were to happen in an orderly fashion. There was no question by this time that growth was accelerating and if safeguards were not in place, a development disaster could happen. All members of the MVCC did not share the same objectives, however. Some were interested in planning and directing growth; some were simply obstructionists; some had environmental goals; others had social goals.

Because Mazama had become a haven for real estate speculators and so much media attention had been devoted to controversy between special interest groups, by the end of the 1970s the area was no longer a secret hideaway. Seattle's daily newspapers carried stories essentially saying that Mazama and the Methow Valley were about to be destroyed. Editorial writers suggested a resort at Mazama would benefit the entire state. Television news people from Spokane and Seattle covered Mazama for features on the proposed resort and the people of the area.

Schools and colleges from all over the Northwest included various perspectives on development of Early Winters in class projects. It was studied in nearly every land-use class, in architecture classes, in public affairs courses, at seminars on community development and was the focus of many a thesis or term paper.

For better or worse, Mazama, Early Winters and the upper Methow Valley were smothered with attention.

But despite all the attention during the 1970s and 1980s and all the real estate sales, the population really didn't grow much. It was sometimes difficult even to get enough able-bodied men to staff the volunteer fire truck. A women's auxiliary was formed to support the firefighters, but it was short-lived. A few summer homes were added. But the number of voters in the Mazama precinct changed very little. Mazama seemed to be in suspension, waiting for something.

The Mazama Store had new owners by the 1970s. They remodeled the front of the building, changed the name to the Mazama Country Store, and enjoyed increasing winter business thanks to the growing popularity of cross-country skiing.

Artist Ron Bomba, a part-time Mazama resident, drew this scene of the golf course, village and ski hill the developers planned for the first phase of the Early Winters Resort.

Chapter 9
The 1980s
The Early Winters Era

The decade of the 1980s can be called the Early Winters Era in the Methow Valley. Real estate was selling like hot cakes in the upper valley and tourism was growing. Anticipation of skiing at Early Winters was the economic generator. People were buying lots for vacation homes and property for subdivision. Young people were moving in with dreams of being part of the resort or starting a business in a prosperous and beautiful environment. Seven real estate offices in Winthrop were all doing well.

For some readers, this chapter will include too much detail about the controversy over the Early Winters Resort and Sandy Butte ski hill plans, but it seems important to chronicle this history because it had such an enormous local impact and led to court decisions that have influenced growth in other parts of the country.

New Arrivals

Dick and Sue Roberts arrived in 1980 with the dream of building a lodge for hikers and skiers. Dick was a handyman and did much of the construction on what the Roberts called the North Cascade Base Camp, which opened in 1981. Sue did the cooking and Dick provided amenities for the guests such as making ski trails with his snowmobile. The Early Winters project allowed him to bridge the river from his property and use the fields and trails it owned. He also built new trails for his guests and the community.

It was about this time that the Methow Valley Ski Trails Association purchased professional ski-trail grooming equipment. Dick Roberts and Don Portman assumed the risks by personally guaranteeing the bank loans necessary to make the organization functional.

'Mr. Fun'

Eric Sanford, a recent transplant from Aspen, Colo., and one of the most upbeat Mazama enthusiasts, brought almost more ideas and activities than Mazama could handle. He billed himself as "Mr. Fun" and set up a business called Liberty Bell Alpine Tours. He sold river rafting trips, backpacking trips, mountaineering and ski tours and kayak lessons. In 1980, Sanford and his friends refurbished the old Stookey/Bowers/Eggelson ranch house, renamed it the Mazama Country Inn and rented rooms to Sanford's clients.

In 1982, Sanford introduced helicopter skiing to the area and gained considerable publicity for Mazama and the North Cascades as a winter sports destination. One success after another led to investment in a new, bigger and better inn and restaurant, which opened in 1984. But business and profits did not keep pace with Sanford's enthusiasm. By 1987, the bank was foreclosing on Sanford and his partners. One of them was Cal Merriman, who ended up buying the inn at a bargain price in a foreclosure sale. Sanford sold his house and property to the Outward Bound Society, took up serious wind surfing and left for the Columbia Gorge as quickly as he had arrived.

As good as things were, the decade was stressful for the Mazama community. Congress finally passed the Washington Wilderness Bill, which made the proposed ski hill at Sandy Butte available for permitting. Methow Recreation Inc., which had applied for the permit, was active and expectations ran high with the cry, "Ski in eighty-three!"

Even with so much attention focused on Early Winters/Mazama, there was very little growth. There were even fewer registered voters in Mazama than in earlier times. Kathy Grimmett, owner of the Mazama store and post office, had to find work outside the valley to subsidize her store to keep it open. Mazama was still in limbo.

Bob and Maryanne Sitts house is located on part of the old Albert Boughey homestead.

Bob and Maryanne Sitts

Bob and Maryanne Sitts arrived in Mazama in 1981 and bought what had been part of HES 85, the homestead of Albert Boughey, the violin maker, and later the site of Harvey Peters sawmill. The Sitts could be considered "old-timers" today, not old-timers as in homesteaders, but old-timers in the sense that they were here before all the "newcomers," and they became an important part of the glue that held Mazama together during a quarter century of controversy and change.

The Sitts are doers. (They were in favor of the ski resort, but did not take an active part in the controversy.) Maryanne and a few others revived the nearly dead Mazama Community Club, which she served as president for a number of years. And she was active in the arts, especially the Northwest Watercolor Society, the local Confluence Galley, and she was a board member of the Methow Music Festival, for which she designed the original logo, and opened her home to the musicians. Bob liked to say it was a full-time job to support Maryanne's activities.

Maryanne and Bob Sitts in front of their barn, where her Kicking Mule Gallery is located.

They both have fascinating backgrounds. Bob's mother died when he was two. His dad was a police officer in Los Angeles at the time so his grandmother came from Seattle to get the boy and raise him. She owned a beauty parlor and barber shop, but after hearing that it was possible to drive a car to the interior of British Columbia, she sold out and they moved into the wilderness. Bob grew up hunting and fishing. He went to a local school with a few neighbor kids and Indian children. But there was no high school and his grandmother was adamant that he must finish high school. So it was back to Seattle.

He served in the Merchant Marine during World War II as a commissioned deck officer after graduating from Kings Point Academy in Kings Point, N.Y. His ship was hit by a torpedo off the British coast, was repaired and sent to the Pacific, where it was torpedoed again off the coast of Mexico and sank. Bob was one of the few to survive. After the war he stayed in the Merchant Marine and sailed the world before marrying and moving to Seattle, where he worked as a private yacht skipper and later for Foss Tug as a pilot and dispatcher. His wife died in 1965. He married Maryanne in 1977.

Maryanne started life on a small farm south of Everett. Her mother died when she was 13, and her father disappeared two years later, so she lived with relatives in Seattle. After high school and a couple years of studying art at the University of Washington, she learned to ski and married a skier and sailor named Bud Magee.

Bud was a sailmaker and boat builder who designed a sailboat that could go 50 mph. They skied and raced sailboats. For 15 years they raced and sailed in England, Bermuda, California, Canada and all around the world. They both learned to fly and owned several planes.

One of the boats they built was a fishing boat purchased by a young man who asked them to help him take it to Alaska to fish for herring. Maryanne was not keen on going, but they talked her into it. By the time they got to Juneau she was suffering from food poisoning and decided to get off the boat and fly home. Bud continued on with the boat owner. The men vanished along with the boat, which apparently capsized.

After losing Bud, Maryanne built an art studio in her home and with five other artists opened a gallery in Seattle's Pioneer Square. After she married Bob Sitts, they lived on a farm near Monroe, but they wanted something else. They looked in Montana, Idaho and Oregon. Maryanne clipped a classified ad from a newspaper that described a piece of property for sale in Mazama. So on the way back from their exploratory tour, they stopped to see the land. It was the spot they wanted.

They built a temporary log cabin, a house and barn. Gate Creek ran through the property, which meant they could generate their own power, something Bob had always wanted to do. They also raised race horses and mules, and Maryanne opened the Kicking Mule Gallery in the barn loft. The Sitts remain a vibrant part of the Mazama community.

A Sad Departure

In March of 1983, Jack Wilson died unexpectedly. He had worked tirelessly for the opening of the North Cascades Highway and was a prime booster for the ski development. Although Wilson kept a string of horses for his Early Winters cabin guests to ride, by then he had converted his trail construction businesses into a trail packing one and sold it to Claude Miller. Off in a new direction after the sale, Wilson purchased a snowmobile and groomed trails at Early Winters for cross-country skiers and his winter guests. When he died, Mazama lost a prominent and beloved citizen.

Enter Harry Hosey

Brian McCauley, who had grown up near Wenatchee but was from an old valley family, was a proponent of the ski resort. As a member of Gov. John Spellman's staff, he had many contacts in government and industry. To help Methow Recreation Inc., McCauley arranged a meeting in 1984 that ended with a merger between MRI and a partnership formed by Harry Hosey of Hosey Engineering. The Hosey firm specialized in the kind of financing and permitting that MRI needed for its Early Winters project.

The Hosey/MRI partnership took over the ski hill project. MRI was the permit applicant, but it was now a wholly-owned subsidiary of the Hosey partnership. Hosey had enjoyed recent success obtaining permits for hydroelectric power projects and was enthusiastic about the prospects for development that Early Winters offered.

The money for the ski hill permit work came from Hosey Engineering, members of the Hosey family and relatives of Harry Hosey's wife Gege. Several hundred thousand dollars were invested up front to hire consultants and attorneys. An additional $1 million was borrowed from the Brennan family (Gege's relatives) as a partial payment to the Aspen Ski Co. for land purchase. Aspen, though no longer interested in the development, had exercised its option and purchased 1,200 acres at Early Winters. Now it wanted to sell, which made negotiations easier, but a considerable cash down payment was required.

The Early Winters Project

The management of Early Winters Resort, the new company, hired Design Workshops Inc., the same planning firm that Aspen had retained to lay out the resort. Project managers spent thousands of dollars to update and expand soil and hydrology studies, wildlife assessments and other environmental studies.

With the passage of the 1984 Washington Wilderness Bill, the Forest Service issued a Final Environmental Impact Statement and Record of Decision to issue the permit for the ski hill at Sandy

The Early Winters Resort logo.

Butte. An appeal by the Methow Valley Citizens Council was received on the last day of the appeal period at the Forest Service office in Twisp. That led to additional friction between Forest Service officials and David Bricklin, attorney for MVCC, about the timing. The Forest Service initially dismissed the appeal, claiming it was postmarked late. But Bricklin, who charged foul play, prevailed.

The chief of the U.S. Forest Service withheld a decision on the MVCC appeal, hoping that the developers and the MVCC could successfully negotiate a settlement. Methow Recreation Inc., the MVCC and Bricklin started negotiating. The Early Winters project manager at that time was Steve Excell, a lawyer and former member of Gov. Spellman's staff. Hours of negotiations and pages of agreements covering the MVCC's social and environmental concerns were compiled. At least two, and sometimes three, members of the negotiating team were lawyers.

After several months, a settlement was reached that the principal members of both sides felt would guarantee environmental safeguards, growth limits and funds for community and environmental purposes. At the signing meeting, however, the MVCC rejected the settlement despite the concessions it had obtained. It appeared as if any individual had veto power over the entire MVCC regardless of what had been agreed to by its negotiators. By then the MVCC had joined forces with Seattle-based environmental groups whose members knew little about the specifics of the controversy. They seemed to oppose the ski resort more as a symbol of development.

A pro-resort bumper sticker.

Mazama Neighbors

During the same time period, another group of valley citizens formed an organization called Mazama Neighbors for the Early Winters Ski Hill. Although founded by Mazama-area landowners, it had valleywide and statewide members and contributors. Directors of the group included Ron Perrow, editor and publisher of the *Methow Valley News*; John Rabel, a Seattle businessman, former legislator and Mazama landowner; and Blair Howe, an Edelweiss homeowner. Howe worked nearly full time for Mazama Neighbors managing the group's fund raising and promotion.

The new group claimed 2,000 members statewide at its peak. The president was Aaron Burkhart, a local rancher. Greydon Patterson, son of a Mazama homesteader, served as vice president. The intent was to make the group genuinely local and grassroots. (Ironically, Aaron Burkhart would later switch sides and bring appeals to delay the project after opponents convinced him he would lose his water rights if the ski hill was built.)

Howe and other members and directors met with opposition groups in an effort to find common ground and to let the media and general public know that there was grassroots support for the resort and ski hill. They ran advertisements in the paper, distributed bumper stickers, issued press releases and held public meetings.

After the MVCC declined to sign the negotiated agreement, Mazama Neighbors held a community meeting in the Winthrop Barn to explain what was happening. They hoped the MVCC would reconsider its decision if they saw there was community support for the ski hill. But the meeting didn't go as planned.

The MVCC members were in no mood to compromise. They attended the meeting to vent. The result was a surge of anti-MVCC sentiment and a polarizing campaign. Almost overnight, "MVCC buster" signs ap-

A pro-resort symbol opposing the Methow Valley Citizens Council's position.

peared on cars, in homes and at businesses in Winthrop and Twisp. Although the Early Winters management had nothing to do with the signs, any atmosphere conducive to negotiation had vaporized.

In 1986 U.S. Forest Service Chief Dale Robertson rejected the MVCC's appeal and issued a permit to Methow Recreation Inc. His decision included a list of requirements aimed at mitigating the concerns of the appellants.

Those requirements covered nearly all the concerns that had been discussed during the negotiations, including air quality, wildlife habitat and employee housing. Also in-

cluded was a requirement that the developers reimburse the county for any costs incurred and that an ongoing tax and assessment on the resort be established to benefit both the county and local community.

While this gave MRI a special use permit for skiing, the organization did not yet have the dozens of permits necessary to built a resort or ski hill, and the permit application for construction had yet to be completed. From 1985 on, permit work was in full swing. Permits were required at the state, local and federal levels and each agency's process and permit application was a major undertaking.

Starting in the mid-1970s, project proponents had worked to see that a proper county zoning ordinance was in place. This was generally complete, but many sub-ordinances had to be in place to comply with the commitments made by the county and the require-

Early Winters managers atop Goat Wall during a planning trip to the resort site. Harry Hosey is on the far right.

ments of the state and Forest Service. For example, to address a perceived threat to deer, a dog control ordinance had to be enacted. To safeguard against possible pollution from off-site developments, an elaborate water quality monitoring system was installed. To prevent air pollution, very sophisticated monitoring procedures were implemented and the most restrictive wood-burning ordinance in the state was adopted.

Every issue and every ordinance was an expensive and time-consuming undertaking that involved public participation. In addition to paying its own staff, the Early Winters company was paying the county for all time and costs incurred. An example of the frustrations experienced by both the developer and the county was the air quality ordinance adopted by the county after the 18th version had been written. Each draft was discussed with the MVCC and that group was given the opportunity to provide input. All of MVCC's requests were included in the 18th version of the ordinance. However, during the final public hearing, Isabelle Spohn, the MVCC air quality spokesperson, testified against the very ordinance she had helped draft.

The proposed tax and assessment plan would have provided considerable revenue for the county, which logically created general support for the project from county and city governments. At this time, nearly every elected official and government entity in North Central Washington supported the project.

However, public support did not daunt the opposition, which by now was headquartered in Seattle and included the Sierra Club and the Washington Environmental Council. These groups brought suit against the Forest Service claiming the Environmental Impact Statement was inadequate. And they started a series of appeals that continued until the U.S. Supreme Court ruled in favor of the Forest Service on May 1, 1989.

However, two issues were not resolved by the court and required additional permit work, which allowed the appellants to begin the whole appeal process again.

Appeals through the federal court system were time-consuming and expensive for Early Winters. Although the opponents appeal was against the Forest Service, the government had minimal resources to carry the case, and MRI acted as an intervening party, picking up a big portion of the legal work and costs. The estimated cost to MRI was nearly $400,000.

David Bricklin was an environmental activist and attorney for the MVCC and the Sierra Club. Despite the Supreme Court ruling in favor of the Forest Service on nearly every issue, Bricklin claimed the unresolved issues allowed him to recover his attorney's fees from the Forest Service under the Equal Access to Justice Act. The EAJA is a federal statute intended to aid small businesses in recovering legal costs if they prevail in a suit against a government agency. Environmental groups successfully have used the EAJA to recover money when they sue the government over environmental issues, and Bricklin claimed the two unresolved issues constituted a victory for him and that he thus was owed more than $200,000 in legal fees. The courts agreed and he collected the fees from the Forest Service.

Two other events occurred at the end of the 1980s that assisted opponents of the Early Winters Resort. One was the creation of an organization called Friends of the Methow, a Puget Sound-based group of environmentalists. Activist representatives from major environmental groups such as the Sierra Club, Audubon Society and Trust for Public Land were part of the Friends organization.

Friends of the Methow, a Seattle-based group of resort opponents, circulated this flyer showing bulldozers denuding the land.

The second event was the federal government's 1990 listing of the Northern spotted owl as a threatened species. Sandy Butte was designated possible owl habitat. Considerable controversy arose over the validity of the scientific evidence submitted to substantiate the habitat claim. However, the owl's status cast a shadow on development until the issue could be resolved, and affected forests and the timber industry throughout the Northwest. Downhill skiing at Early Winters was in limbo. No decisions or appeals were being considered at the time.

Other forces that affected public perception of the resort plan were its size and image. By the end of the 1980s the Early Winters company had spent several million dollars on planning, attorneys, engineers and consultants. In addition, project design work, promised environmental mitigation and safeguards and contributions to social programs in the community added tremendous costs. To cover them, the project was made larger and larger as more demands were made. When the final plans were published, the media reported that the resort would be permitted to include 4,000 housing units and could have as many as 12,000 skiers a day at build-out. This was an exaggerated, worst-case scenario, but it was quite a shock to many in the community. It was not at all what most people had in mind.

At that time, Harry Hosey decided that the project needed to control a number of adjacent acres of Forest Service land for the benefit of the resort, and he proposed a land trade. Because of the urgency Hosey perceived, he sought to bypass the local administrative process by getting direct legislative approval from Congress.

The proposed trade included the Early Winters campground next to Highway 20. Although small and not particularly pretty, it was a campground nonetheless and therefore a "sacred cow" and emotional issue. Opponents made good use of the issue and made getting approval for the trade very difficult and expensive. Hosey succeeded in getting a bill passed that authorized the trade, but the number of conditions attached made it highly unlikely it would ever happen.

Problems in Bellevue

By the late 1980s, the number of partners in the Early Winters Resort project had increased considerably. Hosey was a world-class salesman. He radiated enthusiasm and was never without an answer. He had taken over the roles of project manager, general partner and president, and he raised a couple of million dollars from Puget Sound-area people and from a group in Chicago.

Shortly before this, Hosey hired Judith Shulman, an attorney with a large Seattle firm. She was smart, aggressive and had many contacts among people with funds to invest. Hosey and Shulman were a great team. She had the contacts and Hosey had the product and the sales pitch. She gave the presentations credibility because of her legal background and because she would correct Hosey when he exaggerated too much or wandered too far from the facts.

The new investors were mainly Shulman's contacts. Most of the significant ones in the late 1980s were on the board of directors of the general partner corporation, Early Winters Resort, Inc. Hosey's in-laws, including the Brennan family, were represented by Hosey's brother-in-law, George Chevigny. It was through Chevigny that Hosey recruited Chicago investors.

Shulman recruited several clients, most of whom were involved in real estate as modest developers or investors, who put in about $1 million total. Two of them were on the board of directors. I also was a director and represented the former Methow Recreation Inc. and the Mazama investors group. I provided continuity from the previous studies and knew the technical aspects of the project and site. Shulman acted as secretary and counsel.

Another director was Mary Ferguson, an accountant with a large accounting firm. Ferguson was president of the R.D. Merrill Co., an old timber family firm with large assets in timber, real estate, cash and securities. She managed the Merrill company's funds. Impressed by Shulman's abilities, she was receptive to the presentation Shulman and Hosey made on Early Winters.

There were many third and fourth generation family members among the R.D. Merrill Co. shareholders. Ferguson felt that these young people would be more interested in hearing about an exciting project like Early Winters than they were in listening to reports on board feet of lumber at shareholder meetings. The Early Winters proposal was real estate oriented, secured and required no active management. Hosey appeared to have everything under control, and Ferguson apparently thought completing the permit process was only a formality. Thus the Merrill Company invested $300,000 in the project and guaranteed a loan for $4 million secured by the property. Ferguson was added to the board of directors as a non-voting member.

In the boardroom in Bellevue, Washington, everything seemed great. Hosey hired

This version of the proposed resort from the Harry Hosey days was to have a compact village at its core with commercial businesses on the first floor and residential units above. The architectural style was to be similar to traditional national park buildings constructed with logs and other natural materials.

Norb Valley to be project manager. He was an accountant who had been a financial officer for a firm developing the Hilton Waikoloa resort on the Big Island of Hawaii. Hosey moved Valley to Seattle from southern California, bought him a new car and started him at twice the salary of any previous manager or employee. After six months, Hosey realized Valley was not the man for the job and paid to move him to Texas, where he had wanted to go in the first place. Hosey made himself project manager. He worked harder than ever attempting to manage every little detail.

With all the new money available, Hosey spent at record rates – charter flights to the Methow Valley, dinners for local citizens, a directors' trip to Florida to see a Disney hotel and a move to brand new, spacious office quarters large enough to triple the staff. The office was complete with custom-made furniture that cost thousands of dollars and a conference table built by Hosey's brother Bernie Hosey, a metal sculptor. Consultants from every imaginable discipline were hired. Staff people assigned to work with the consultants said they were finding their jobs difficult to manage because Hosey continually meddled in their work, changing instructions and directions.

Hosey was going at a frenzied pace, doing almost everything himself. A public relations firm was hired to write a newsletter, but Hosey insisted on either writing it himself or rewriting what the professionals wrote. Although the best consultants were hired, if they didn't say what Hosey wanted to hear, they were phased out. The attorneys, the public relations firm, and the planner all were replaced.

By the end of the 1980s, Shulman had quit practicing law and set herself up as a consultant at hourly rates. She worked nearly full time for Hosey on the Early Winters project and traveled everywhere with him. His marriage soon was on the rocks.

The Hosey Engineering Co. also was falling apart, partly because Hosey had been its best and main salesman and he was no longer there, and partly because he tried to manage it from afar. The employees gave Hosey an ultimatum: sell the company to someone who can run it or we'll leave. The company was sold to Harza, a large Chicago firm.

Hosey had invested the engineering firm's funds in the Early Winters project from the beginning; those were the funds that got the project off the ground in 1985. For this, the company had been issued ownership in Early Winters. Neither Harza nor the old employees wanted this asset. Hosey did, and so he received it as partial settlement for giving up his ownership in the engineering company.

On the brighter side, by 1990 Hosey, the staff and consultants had put together an impressive resort plan. Early Winters unquestionably would be the most elaborate and complete resort in the state. Considerable market research showed great demand for the resort as planned. Phase one of the project was projected to be very successful from a sales point of view. Everything from ski lifts to golf course irrigation was to be state-of-the-art. There was nothing like it in the state.

If revenues met the projections done by state agencies, the county and the state would prosper from the increased tax base and increased economic activity by the second year of the resort's operation. By the end of the third year, both the state and the county would receive a surplus over costs of services from projected business and state excise taxes.

In addition, the U.S. Forest Service permit required a payback of two percent of ski lift revenues into a county-administered program to be used for local public transportation or anything else the community felt was important. Many felt that the resort would be a win-win deal for government and the developers. However, two big "ifs" remained: obtaining the permits to allow the project to happen, and raising money to pay for it.

Jerry Blann Returns

In 1990, Jerry Blann, who had been running a resort in California, reappeared on the scene with another attempt to bring investment money and management to the Early Winters Resort project. He had left Aspen some years before and he and an associate, Ron Miller, had made an unsuccessful effort to buy the ski area at Breckenridge, Colo.

Miller had been president and CEO of the Disney Co. and retained the dream of Walt Disney, his father-in-law, to create a picturesque mountain village. Disney had tried to develop the Mineral King area in California but was stopped by environmental groups. Miller was impressed with the Early Winters plan. His site visit started a series of meetings aimed at getting him involved and of having Blann become project manager.

Blann had expertise in the ski industry and knew the details of Early Winters. He'd lived on the site for two years and had done much of the preliminary development work on the mountain. All of the Early Winters Resort, Inc., directors felt he was an ideal solution for many of the project's problems.

But when the directors' objective of having Blann become CEO of the project became clear to Hosey, he scuttled the negotiations and took on the board. Staff, consultants, and even government agency people working with the project were aware of the management problems. Okanogan County staffers were downright angry with Hosey. Some

Forest Service employees were so irritated they rolled their eyes at the mere mention of his name.

By this time Hosey's estranged wife Gege had become concerned about her family's investment. Her fears were confirmed by her brother George, who was on the board. Hosey had invested not only his wife's inheritance but also their community property. This resulted in a messy divorce and struggle for control of the project management, which took much of Hosey's time. On the advice of her lawyer, Gege gave Hosey the right to vote the shares of their community property. With his new control, Hosey removed three of the five board members. I was ousted along with his brother-in-law George.

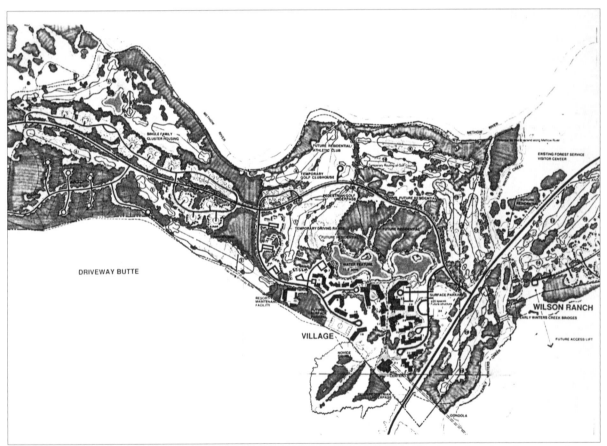

The Early Winters Resort plan proposed in 1990 designated part of the golf course for the Wilson Ranch area and part on the present Early Winters Campground.

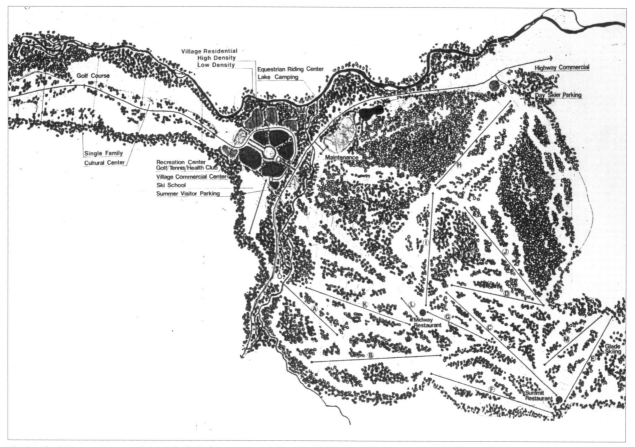

The Early Winters Resort plan included this proposed downhill ski area layout for Sandy Butte. Lift Number 1 was a gondola.

This sign made by Eric Burr depicts the "new" Mazama as a recreational paradise. The sign framework was originally built by Jack Wilson and was located a mile west of the entrance to his Early Winters Cabins.

Chapter 10

The 1990s
A Thriving Economy and a New Plan for Early Winters

Recreation and tourism were without question the main economic engines in Mazama and the upper Methow Valley by the 1990s. The Methow Valley Ski Touring Association was grooming trails for cross-country skiers throughout the Early Winters property and Mazama with connecting trails that went to Winthrop and into the Rendezvous area to the Chewuch River.

The Mazama Country Inn was providing quality accommodations and good meals for skiers. Cal Merriman, who purchased HES 114, was operating the inn and had developed a large arena and horse riding facility as well. There was calf roping throughout the summer with special instructors brought in to teach roping. Merriman and other investors were planning a major subdivision called Chechaquo for the remainder of HES 114.

Although it appeared to be a lazy agricultural community because few houses were built, in reality Mazama had been subdivided through the years. There were more than 900 lots above the Weeman Bridge.

In the late 1980s, the community of Mazama, fearing uncontrolled growth even with the existing county zoning ordinance, produced a master plan for development of the commercial area. There was consensus that too much land was designated commercial, which would lead to a sprawled, highway-oriented town. The majority of citizens expressed a desire for a compact pedestrian-oriented town off the main state highway. The county adopted the master plan drafted by the community. The commercial area wasn't as small as many people desired, but in general, most people felt it was better than having no plan at all.

The MVSTA trail system continued to gain so much momentum in the 1990s that the organization's name was changed from Methow Valley Ski Touring Association to Methow Valley Sport Trails Association to reflect the trail systems all-season use. The community began to see the value of the trail system, particularly for attracting tourists. Helicopter skiing out of Mazama had been introduced in the 1980s, and together with skiing on machine-groomed trails, Mazama gained a national reputation as one of the country's pre-eminent winter sports destinations.

A Tireless Dreamer

John Hayes, who like many people moved to the valley from Aspen, Colorado, when the Aspen Skiing Co. was proposing an alpine ski development in Mazama, was behind much of the momentum. Hayes had been involved in a number of business deals in Aspen. Now he was immersed in community activities in the Methow Valley, including the dream of creating a public trail from Winthrop to Lost River with miles of side loops for skiing, hiking, bicycling and horseback riding. Because many miles of private property would have to be crossed, few thought it could work. However, John, a tireless dreamer with unlimited energy, was determined to make the trail system a reality and he did. He contacted many of the property owners personally and got Lee Miller, a local realtor and friend involved. Over time, the trail became reality.

John Hayes moved to Mazama from Colorado, and immersed himself in community activities.

John is a veteran of the U.S. Marine Corps who served in Vietnam, where he was wounded by three gunshots and an exploding grenade. He lost his left eye, but not an ounce of his enthusiasm for life. After his first visit to the Methow in 1974, John and his wife Rayma spent several years traveling the world, sailing and working at various jobs.

They returned to the valley in 1983 and started the Little Star Montessori School in Winthrop. Rayma ran the school while John got involved in assisting people with land development. John had a penchant for being in the middle of every happening in the community. He wanted to help, he wanted to run it, he wanted to be the authority and he wanted to influence, all of which resulted in hours of conversation and discussion. He made many contributions to the community, donated hours of service to various causes, and took on challenges, undaunted by lack of time or resources. John continues to devote energy to valley projects.

The Olympians Arrive

The proposed Early Winters ski resort had brought a wave of newcomers, but even after the plan's demise, settlers arrived in numbers. At least two of them were Olympians. Laura Mueggler McCabe and Leslie Thompson Hall, both members of the U.S. Olympic Cross-Country Ski Team, settled in Mazama with their families in 1996.

Laura was born in Bozeman, Montana. Her father was a grasslands scientist for the U.S. Forest Service who was transferred to Logan, Utah, when Laura was in third grade. She grew up as a downhill skier, but also was a competitive runner who attended the University of Utah on a distance-running scholarship. By her senior year she was tired

Two elite skiers moved to Mazama in the 1990s, former Olympian Laura Mueggler McCabe, on left, carrying her daughter Dashe, and Leslie Thompson Hall, two-time Olympian and former national champion, on the right, holding her daughter Ella.

of running but still loved competition. She took up cross-country ski racing, and in 1991 competed in the national championships. By 1994, she was named to the U.S. Olympic Team.

By then she had married Sean McCabe, an art student she met at the University of Utah. He was a skier and climber, the son of a military family who had been born in San Diego but lived all over the country. He got hooked on climbing, which took him to the Himalayas and other destinations in Asia, before he settled in Park City, Utah, near his brother, and went back to school.

In 1995, the U.S. Cross-Country Ski Team went to Sweden to train for six months. Laura didn't want to leave her husband and didn't go. But in 1998 she again made the U.S. team and went to the Olympics in Japan. Sean was teaching art in a Salt Lake City school at the time.

By then, the McCabes felt Park City was becoming too urban. They wanted to start a family in a more rural setting that had skiing and climbing. They heard about the Methow Valley, visited on a weekend, bought a lot in Edelweiss and moved here in 1996. Sean built their house. Laura did odd jobs and helped coach the fledgling cross-country ski program. Later, Sean became an art teacher at Liberty Bell Junior/Senior High School in Winthrop, where he is much praised as a gifted teacher. The couple continues to pursue competitive skiing.

Leslie was originally from Stowe, Vermont, a famous New England ski resort town, and she loved cross-country ski racing. She went to Dartmouth College, which is well-known for turning out top ski racers. She was named to the National Cross-Country Ski Development Team in the early 1980s, an achievement and honor that recognized her skills.

A teammate from Aspen, Colorado, told her about the proposed Early Winters resort in Mazama and said he was planning to move there to work for the Aspen Ski Corp. Sometime later, Leslie was in Park City, Utah, the headquarters for the U.S. Ski Team, and her teammate Laura McCabe told her she was planning to move to Mazama but asked her not to tell anybody.

After Leslie quit racing in 1995, she met Alex Hall, the brother of one of her former teammates, in Park City. Alex also was from Vermont, had attended the University of Vermont and was a dedicated alpine skier. After college he had worked on building and remodeling jobs in Alaska and Seattle and continued to ski. Neither Leslie nor Alex wanted to live in a city, so they decided to visit their friends the McCabes, who by now were living in Mazama. Leslie and Alex got married and bought a lot next door to their friends.

Alex started building houses. Leslie worked at Jack's Hut and Mazama Mountaineering. She got active in coaching and involved with the Nordic Club's annual ski clinic, which draws 100 participants and has a waiting list to attend. She continues to coach, race and raise a family.

Alex took up cross-country skiing after they moved to Mazama and is now an avid racer. He was able to beat Leslie occasionally when she was having children, but now that she is back in top form, that isn't likely to happen again.

This swimming pool was one of many amenities added to the Mazama Country Inn in the 1990s by its new owners.

Inn Has New Owners

The Mazama Country Inn was purchased by Bill Pope and George Turner in 1994. George had practiced law, taught philosophy at Evergreen College and worked for the state legislature. The two men had been good friends when they were in law school at the University of Washington. They loved the outdoors, especially hiking and back-country skiing, and thought owning the inn would be a great adventure.

Bill's connection to the Methow Valley was through his father, who was one of six doctors from Group Health Cooperative in Seattle who had purchased a number of ranches in the Lucky Jim and Hancox Creek areas as an investment. Bill spent summer vacation time in the valley in the late 1970s and had great memories.

After high school, Bill went to Yale University, then finished his legal education at the University of Washington School of Law. He practiced law at a large Seattle firm that did work for Microsoft. From 1986 to 1996, he was Microsoft's in-house counsel. Like many others who became landowners in Mazama during that time period, he was a benefactor of Microsoft's generous stock plan and the stock was skyrocketing.

Bill had the money to buy the inn his friend George would manage. They called their partnership an "excellent adventure," and embarked on an expansion plan that included four more guest rooms, a tennis court, swimming pool and exercise facility with a squash court and sauna. They also formed the Mazama Athletic Club, open to local residents.

Everything was going great. Bill built a vacation home across the road and purchased the only commercial building in Mazama. He opened a gallery in one part of it. But by 2004, George had had enough of the "excellent adventure." He moved back to the west side of the Cascades. He continues to be an absentee landlord, but a longtime Mazama resident, Mary Milka, is the manager. Mary started her life in Mazama in 1977 as manager of the Mazama Store.

Early Winters in the 1990s

By 1991 it was clear that Harry Hosey was not going to continue with the Early Winters project. This was a "good news, bad news" situation. Some of those working on the project looked forward to a fresh start with new management. The bad news was that probably all, or most, investors would lose the money and time they had invested so far. There also was a fear, both in and outside the community, that the property would be divided and sold off as quickly as possible. The result would be dozens of small developers and speculators chopping the land into the maximum number of parcels with virtually no plan, all to the detriment of the community. Most agreed, including the most responsible Seattle environmental groups, that this would be a tragedy.

John Hayes had been working with members of some Seattle environmental groups and had been honored for his work on trail development. With the idea that I might be able to help direct, or at least influence, future ownership of the land, John brought representatives of several environmental groups to the Methow Valley for numerous meetings with me. Various alternatives and strategies were discussed, including establishing a trust, developing a scaled-down version of the project and purchasing land to put into a conservancy.

After Harold Heath's successful sale of the 800-acre Big Valley Ranch to the state, Hayes and others, such as representatives from the Trust for Public Land, were optimistic that something similar could be put together for the Early Winters property. (It happened about five years later.)

The year 1992 was ushered in by R. D. Merrill making another interest payment on the note it was guaranteeing for Early Winters and starting foreclosure proceedings. Those proceedings were not publicly known, but some people were suspicious. Many creditors had not been paid and the project owed the county $30,000 for a preliminary sewer study.

At this time, the Northern spotted owl issue surfaced again. Sandy Butte was considered possible owl habitat, which could put it off-limits to most development. However, no owls had been found for several years and evidence that any spotted owls had ever been found there was questionable at best.

The Forest Service proposed that the Sandy Butte area be traded for another area where owls actually had been found. That area was not classified and was slated for logging. The Forest Service proposal took Seattle-area environmental groups, such as the Sierra Club and Washington Environmental Council, among others, somewhat by surprise, and they reacted quickly with arguments stating why this would not work. They enlisted the Sierra Club Legal Defense Fund and hinted at legal action if the proposal were pursued. Their position was that not only was the idea of trading unacceptable, but also that the non-classified area must promptly be added to the protected habitat.

Not wanting heat from the environmental community, Forest Service officials abandoned the idea of a trade. Sandy Butte was declared a possible Habitat Conservation Area on the basis of evidence that was less than compelling. In December 1991, the *Methow Valley News* reported owl sightings in detail. The article included the following sentence: "Teams of temporary Forest Service staff, often college students, were trained in a 24-hour-long Northern Spotted Owl Inventory & Monitoring workshop."

The following verbatim transcript of field notes recorded during a 24-hour period by a 1988 study team was used to establish the presence of a pair of spotted owls on Sandy Butte:

" * *May 27, 1988: 2050 – saw owl (fly over heads) not a GHO (Great Horned Owl), pygmy or screech. Prob barred or spotted.*

* June 28, 1988: 2119 hrs – owl visual – no call – medium size

* 2301 hrs – unknown owl presumed a spotted – 1st 3 notes good – far away"

More trips were made on July 18 and 19 and on August 3, with no visual sightings except: *"sighted bird fly across road and then back."* Many felt that these field notes call into question whether the criteria were met to designate the area a spotted owl habitat. The Forest Service said in 1991 that "since 1988 additional survey work has not produced any evidence of the existence of Northern spotted owls on Sandy Butte."

Some Forest Service staffers believed that while clear-cut logging was not good for owl habitat, skiing probably was not a threat to them, even if they were present. The entire owl issue was quite emotional, very political and governed by rules that seemed to change weekly. Forest Service officials pleaded for time to work out the dilemma, but Hosey viewed the owl issue as a deal buster. He had been unsuccessful in raising funds and the owl may have been a convenient scapegoat.

According to Hosey, he was unable to raise money because the "owl put a cloud over the project." Forest Service officials, and most of the partners who were informed, regarded the owl as just another issue to be solved like the water, sewer or air quality issues, but it appeared Hosey used it to rationalize his failure to raise funds. The press carried Hosey's story in local and Seattle papers. This irritated Forest Service officials as well as most of the partners because such publicity potentially was damaging to the project and adversely affected the value of the real estate.

In retrospect, Hosey probably was right. The owl was a deal buster. The issue never was resolved. The Forest Service, after losing many battles with environmental groups apparently did not have the stomach to continue the fight. Close examination of the evidence of owl sightings on Sandy Butte would not likely have stood up to scrutiny and would have ended up being an embarrassment to the agency. The Forest Service biologists who would have had to justify the designation as habitat probably were relieved when Hosey ran out of money to challenge them.

By the end of January 1992, R.D. Merrill officials realized the company was headed for ownership of Early Winters through foreclosure. The company faced a dilemma. It could foreclose, which would adversely affect the project, or it could delay foreclosure and allow Hosey to get into a deeper mess. Company officials decided to post public notice of foreclosure on February 3.

Steve Devin carves turns in the spring snow on Sandy Butte.

On August 7, 1992, all assets of the Early Winters project were to be sold to the highest bidder in a foreclosure sale on the Okanogan County Courthouse steps. (Actually, the sale was moved to the basement because a strong wind was blowing.) Several members of the media attended the sale, along with several MVCC activists and a handful of people who claimed an interest in bidding. However, no bids were made other than the $800,000 bid from the R.D. Merrill representative.

The company had guaranteed a $4 million loan and had been making interest payments of about $10,000 per month for several months. The other shareholders, including Merrill – which had made several last-gasp loans to Hosey in an attempt to keep the project alive – stopped advancing funds. Merrill thus had about $4.5 million plus $300,000 in equity in the project. After foreclosure, all it had was the land and a Piston Bully snow groomer. The rest of the partners were washed out completely, losing several million dollars. A number of suppliers and some employees were left unpaid, in an aggregate sum of about $400,000.

The Lowe Development Company

At about the time that Early Winters was trying to get permits, the proposed Point Defiance Resort near Sequim, Washington, on the Olympic Peninsula also was in trouble. The resort was being financed by Mitsubishi, a large Japanese firm, but economic conditions were causing it to reassess its overseas investments. Mitsubishi pulled out. Lowe Development Co. of California was doing the work for Mitsubishi with Andy Norris in charge. Lowe had been operating in the Pacific Northwest for 20 years and had done market research in the area. The company's conclusion was that Washington was under-supplied with resorts.

The Jerry Hillis law firm in Seattle was working on the Sequim project. They kept informed on the situation at Early Winters because I occasionally met with them on a friendship basis. Glenn Amster, who had been the partner most familiar with Early Winters, set up a meeting for me with Norris that resulted in a preliminary meeting with the Merrill Co.

Cordy Wagner, Merrill board chairman, and Bagley Wright, a wealthy Seattle businessman whose wife Ginnie is a Merrill, listened to what Norris had to say. Impressed, they hired the Lowe Co. to come up with a recommendation for how to proceed and eventually to manage the project.

Norris had followed the Early Winters project over the years and had liked it. The Northwest was one of the Lowe Co.'s three most desirable spots in the country for building a resort. Norris came from a ski resort background. He had considerable experience with development in Vail, but he was concerned about the capital required to build a major ski resort given the Early Winters situation. He and others envisioned a scaled-down resort for the Early Winters property modeled after the Black Butte or Sunriver resorts in Oregon.

At this point, the Hillis law firm was back in the picture temporarily, looking out for the interests of the Merrill Co., and Bill Pettit replaced Ferguson as president of the firm. Pettit and Norris started the whole process over again, from feasibility through design, with the entire environmental approval process taking years of time and hundreds of thousands of dollars. Norris was undaunted by the environmental challenges, but the banker, Pettit, saw continuing problems and massive costs. Despite his views, a former planner from Vail, Peter Patten, was hired to manage planning for a resort.

In August 1993 the Merrill family, including all the company shareholders, had their annual gathering in the Methow Valley to look over their new holdings. They stayed and played at Sun Mountain, toured the Early Winters site and had a picnic in Shafer Field below Goat Wall. The weather was delightfully warm, the sky clear and a small stream trickled over the falls on the rock wall. It was gorgeous and impressive. Of the approximately 15 family members present, only a couple were not supportive of the company being involved with a resort in this spectacular setting. This gathering, and a 1994 meeting at Sunriver with Wagner and Wright, probably were pivotal in the decision-making process.

About this same time, Lowe got involved in a large development and acquisition project at Sunriver, which made Early Winters a part-time assignment for Norris. Things moved very slowly for many months. Much of the previous work was repeated but new work also was undertaken.

One aspect of the project was given major attention – communication with opponents of the earlier project. Norris and Pettit met with various groups of valley people from numerous locations, businesses and social circles to get a feel for what the community wanted to have happen at Early Winters. Norris excelled at these public meetings. He said all the right things and the community felt the project was in good hands.

In addition to local people, Norris met with Ron Judd, leader of the Seattle-based Friends of the Methow. Judd owned real estate in the valley and thus had more than the typical environmentalist's view of the situation. He was also a pragmatic labor official with influence in nearly all environmental groups as well as state government. It was felt that if anyone could bring about reasoned discussion and a practical solution, it was Judd.

Out of Norris' meeting with Judd came an agreement for Judd and FOM to work informally for the development of the project, but only if the existence of the agreement remained confidential. In exchange, the developers would agree to the following five points:

* No alpine skiing
* No land exchange
* No Mazama sewer
* Merrill Co. support for an environmental center
* The MVCC would have the right to buy the land if no project was built.

With this agreement accomplished, the company's attention was turned to the environmental groups, and, as a result, communication with mainstream Methow people and previous supporters of the project came to an abrupt halt.

Merrill Co. officials apparently felt that the confidential agreement prevented them from meeting with others. When Merrill took over the project, the company was regarded as a "white knight," but with lack of attention to the community, that image began to slip. From a practical point of view, Merrill didn't need the community because it would not actively oppose the project. The company's attention was focused on those interested in stopping the development or threatening Merrill with legal action.

One of the issues that seemed important to FOM was building an environmental center. To this end, Merrill and Peter Goldman, vice president of the Kongsgaard-Goldman Foundation, each put up $25,000 to explore the feasibility of the center. Goldman and his wife Martha Kongsgaard are committed to supporting environmental and human rights work through their foundation. They also love the Methow Valley and purchased the former Gunn Ranch as a vacation home.

Tom Robinson was head of the Washington Environmental Council in Seattle. He also was married to Maggie Coon, a strong opponent of Early Winters development and the ski area. Politically astute and a reasonable negotiator, Robinson was hired to do the resort's environmental study and work with various factions in the environmental community. Despite his successes, he worked at the task for less than a year before leaving the job and area.

Meanwhile, Patten was in Seattle sifting through scientific and environmental studies and grinding out a plan and an EIS that complied with the ever-changing results of negotiations. Work in 1994 resulted in a permit application being submitted and some turned dirt near the Early Winters cabins. Lowe was not interested in the cabins, so a group of Merrill family members financed that portion of the project.

Lowe and Merrill had not yet actually signed an agreement or formed their partnership, so Merrill was still the owner of the land and the project. The company was in the asset management and timber businesses. It had done some real estate investing and development, but nothing on the scale of Early Winters. It was a quiet and conservative company that didn't like controversy. It was obvious there would be a number of surprises in store.

One surprise came when Merrill started remodeling Jack Wilson's old Early Winters cabins. The company had been advised by local builders to take a low-profile approach to the remodel. However, Merrill selected James Cutler, of Cutler Anderson Architects, an award-winning Seattle architect who had co-designed Microsoft founder Bill Gates' multi-million dollar house. Perhaps the company thought the firm's credentials would impress local rural officials and expedite the issuance of permits.

The architects met with the county planning office representative and a state shorelines official who were briefed in detail on the firm's experience, creative environmental ideas and what was happening in the world outside the Methow. The county officials were not impressed and dug in their heels. Nothing seemed to happen for months.

The county could not seem to deal with the issue in a reasonable way. Merrill's response was to turn the matter over to the company's attorney. This caused a minor, but expensive, standoff with the county attorney, who finally relented and allowed work to proceed.

It appeared that Merrill either had no marketing plan or that it did not intend to target families, as the cabin owners always had done. The popular four-person cabins were converted to one-bedroom units. To some, a cozy country cabin atmosphere was replaced with an eclectic interior of uncomfortable furniture ill-suited for families or groups. When the cabins finally opened for business, occupancy fell to a fraction of the previous rates. However, it is only fair to note that a big portion of the previous cabin business was generated because of the rates, which were about half those for the remodeled cabins.

As part of the overall product mix of the completed resort, the cabins undoubtedly would fit a niche in the market. But as an opening product, the community was not overly impressed. On the next go-round with the Wilson ranch, the lodges and the inn, things were much different and the community was impressed.

Charlie Wright and Arrowleaf

Another significant event happened in 1994 with the addition of Charlie Wright to the development team. Charlie is Bagley and Virginia Wright's son, and his mother is a direct descendant of R.D. Merrill. The elder Wrights are well known as patrons of the arts in the Seattle area. Charlie Wright had been an attorney with the Hillis law firm but left to work in arts promotion, and the administration of arts foundations in New York. He was lured back to the Northwest to take over the family business partially by the challenge of developing the land at Early Winters. While this was only a small part of the company's enterprises, it was nonetheless an interesting challenge.

As it turned out, Wright was the right person for the job. With his legal background, familiarity with land use law and his personal belief in environmental awareness, he was well equipped to jump into the negotiations process. Wright was soft-spoken, a good listener and had a way of letting people know that he understood what they were saying. Folks felt he would seriously address their concerns.

About this time the project was renamed Arrowleaf, after the Arrowleaf balsamroot daisy that blooms in abundance in the Methow Valley in spring. (Some say Methow is the Indian name for the daisy.)

After two years of nearly non-stop meetings, the Methow Valley Citizens Council and Friends of the Methow signed a memorandum of understanding regarding the development of the Wilson Ranch. Most members of these groups felt the development plan for the overall project was the best proposal that had been submitted. While the Early Winters resort proposal had asked for a maximum build-out of 4,000 units, this one asked for only about 600. The directors of MVCC had spent a lot of time discussing details of the project and Merrill had conceded to nearly every request. For example:

   * Merrill agreed to have no ski hill and to put restrictions on the land to forever prevent it from being used by downhill skiers.

Charlie Wright in 1996 at the completion of the first phase Wilson Ranch project.

   * Merrill reduced the density from the legally allowed 3.5 units per acre to 0.8 units per acre.

   * Mazama residents and neighboring properties would not be allowed to hook up to the project's sewage treatment facilities. This would prevent or hinder further development at Mazama.

   * Because the name Early Winters was so widely known and acted as such an economic generator, it would not be used.

   * MVCC would be intimately involved in planning and development.

   * The developer would assist in funding a full-time environmental institute, which also would have long-term funding for environmental projects in other parts of the valley.

The agreement split the environmental groups. The original understanding was that the plan would be approved by the environmentalists in segments. However, state law would not permit a phased EIS. It had to be done all at once. The Methow Valley Citizens Council found this unacceptable. However, the Friends of the Methow, and others from Seattle more experienced with the law and its goals, understood and accepted the situation. Thus an agreement was reached for the Wilson Ranch portion of the Early Winters property. The MVCC never did sign onto this, or any other agreement, for the remainder of the project. Nevertheless, meetings continued and project managers attempted to comply with both the details and the spirit of the agreement.

While the negotiations that led to the agreement were going on, a number of environmentally conscious people were "discovering the Methow." They wanted to be involved, but had to get up to speed on the issues and learn what had been accomplished. The MVCC president and most of the board members resigned, exhausted. Thus the group was taken over by enthusiastic new people who were ready to save the environment of the valley they had just discovered.

The Okanogan Wilderness League (OWL), also came on the scene. The group's membership appeared to consist of two people, Lee "Bernie" Bernheisel and Lucy Reid, enthusiastic anti-growthers. They appeared to devote themselves nearly full time to trying to stop development by arguing that in-stream water flows are the primary water right. They have had some success in disrupting growth in the town of Twisp by suing the town over the expansion of its water system. They also delayed completion of the Merrill/Wilson Ranch project. And they cost Arrowleaf tens of thousands of dollars by contesting the development's water rights by appealing state agency decisions that recognized those water rights.

But not all the delays and obstructions in the developer's path can be credited to environmentalists. Agency bureaucrats found innumerable opportunities to cause slowdowns. Numerous agencies are involved in large and visible projects like Arrowleaf. They must be informed and sign off, issue permits, or take some action either for the EIS or for construction.

When the state issued the water permit for the Wilson Ranch, Bernheisel and Reid appealed it. All agencies stopped work on the overall project. Nearly all of them claimed to be overloaded with work and any reason to lighten the load was embraced. In the case of Arrowleaf, the agencies apparently regarded the appeal as an injunction and stopped work. Even the county stopped work. The head of each agency had to be contacted, the attorney general had to become involved and the year was nearly over before progress resumed.

Despite these obstacles, the plan and the EIS were completed in 1995. After they were issued, the public had an opportunity to attend hearings and submit comments. The year 1996 was well under way by the time changes were made to reflect public comment and the county's requests.

Arrowleaf wins county approval

❏ *25 years after first plan, Mazama resort gets go-ahead*

by Lee Hicks

Okanogan county commissioners have approved a preliminary development plan for Arrowleaf resort, decades after the first blueprints were drawn for the site in the upper Methow Valley.

In a unanimous decision on Aug. 20, the commissioners voted to rezone 1,208 acres near Mazama to permit construction of a year-round resort that includes an 18-hole golf course, 690 dwelling units divided between lodge rooms, single family homes and condominiums, and a retail village.

"We want to express our appreciation to the county commissioners and the planning staff," said Merrill CEO Charlie Wright after hearing the decision. "They gave careful review to the plan and committed an incredible amount of time during the process."

Tuesday's decision follows last week's denial by the commissioners of an appeal by Methow Valley Citizens Council which argued that the environmental impact statement for the project was inadequate.

In approving the preliminary proposal for Arrowleaf, the commissioners stipulated a number of conditions that the development group, R. D. Merrill Co. and Lowe Development Resorts, must address as construction proceeds.

A priority concern has been maintaining air quality in the upper Valley. The preliminary development plan included a proposal for 239 wood-burning devices, with a review process to kick in after 81 devices were in operation.

After considering their options, the commissioners decided to require a performance review after only 40 wood-

---

"We want to express our appreciation to the county commissioners and the planning staff. They gave careful review to the plan and committed an incredible amount of time during the process."
Merrill CEO, Charlie Wright

Part of an article from the Aug. 22, 1996, issue of the Methow Valley News

The Freestone Inn Opens

In July of 1996, the Arrowleaf project opened the Freestone Inn, a beautiful lodge at Wilson Ranch with 12 luxury rooms and a small dining room. The idea was to show the community the quality and sensitivity the developers intended to carry throughout the resort. However, the rest of the project still was being protested. In September, after rejecting the MVCC's appeal contesting the adequacy of the EIS, the Okanogan County Commissioners approved plans for the complete Arrowleaf resort.

The MVCC responded by filing an appeal of the commissioners' decision in the last hours of the day in adjoining Chelan County. Among issues the appeal raised were that the EIS failed to cover all issues and that the EIS was too long. Would the many controversial issues ever be resolved?

When the first edition of this book was being completed in 1996, Harbor Properties, a Seattle development firm, was replacing Lowe as the development partner at Arrowleaf. Harbor Properties primarily is owned by the Bullitt family, which has an old timber legacy. The company is active in environmental causes. It appeared that Harbor Properties development experience and environmental sensitivity would provide a good partner for the R.D. Merrill Co.

Nevertheless, the MVCC's appeal of a technical point on the adequacy of the Environmental Impact Statement was still pending. The fate of the Arrowleaf project wasn't known although opening day for the resort seemed more certain.

As the 1990s came to a close, Mazama was a bustling country crossroads. The community had seen the opening of a new store, a remodel of the old Mazama Ranch House, expanded tourist accommodations and many new housing starts. But there still were more deer than people. And the people were still complaining about the bears in their apple trees, the winters that arrive too early, the bitter cold and heavy snow, the river that dries up almost every year and the fishing that just isn't what it used to be – complaints that probably have been made for the past 100 years.

Phase one of the Arrowleaf Resort development included building today's Freestone Inn and restaurant on the edge of a small lake made from an old gravel quarry. Jack Wilson allowed the state to dig the quarry on his land with a lake in mind, although he couldn't get it to hold water. The Merrill Company lined the hole to prevent leakage, stocked it with fish and used it to store water for irrigation.

Vacation homes. Retirement homes. Investment homes. An unprecedented construction boom ushered in the new century in Mazama.

Chapter 11
The 2000s
A Booming Mazama Enters
A New Century

There probably are as many reasons as people to explain why newcomers settle in Mazama. It's not a very convenient place. The climate is harsh. It is not easy living. It doesn't provide protection from invading hordes or armies – all reasons people have historically gathered or settled in certain locations.

Gold and free land were the magnets at the turn of the 20th century. Most of those who passed through or settled here were searching for gold or supporting those who were searching for it; others lusted after land of their own. One hundred years later, at the turn of the 21st century, the draws were natural beauty and recreation.

There wasn't much more fanfare in Mazama for the Millenium than there had been at the dawn of the 1900s, but there were some noteworthy differences in how people lived. For one thing, there was electric power on New Year's Eve, and most homes had television sets that showed what was happening outside Mazama. For another, even with deep snow, it was usually possible to leave Mazama if one so chose. But other than a few modern conveniences, it wasn't all that different.

At the beginning of both centuries, people were concerned about natural resources and development, albeit from different perspectives. As the 20th century dawned, life was consumed by attempts to clear land, provide food and shelter and develop a community. Staying employed was a challenge and often meant trying to find or mine gold or log the forest.

By 2000, figuring out how to provide food and shelter was not nearly as challenging as deciding how to preserve fish stocks, expand recreational opportunities and slow the pace of development.

There were plenty of jobs in the upper valley as the new century began. In fact, most businesses had "Help Wanted" signs posted.

The first Mazama store, run by Lucille and Homer Peters, has been moved about and recycled several times. It sat next to the barn at the Mazama Ranch House for several decades and served as a bunkhouse, then a storehouse. Moved to its present "city center" location, it became the Burnt Finger Bar-B-Q restaurant. Today it is headquarters for North Cascades Mountain Guides.

The Mazama Community Club is another building that dates back to the early days. It started life as the "new" schoolhouse.

Recreation is a High Priority

Work is not a high priority for most full-time Mazama residents, and if it is necessary to bring in a little income, work is kept to a bare minimum. Part time jobs and short work weeks are the norm. Retirees and owners of vacation homes used part time have joined those who work and live here for the recreational opportunities and lifestyle.

Mazama resident Bob Sitts once observed that most of the cars and vans in Mazama have roof racks that can carry every imaginable piece of recreational equipment – skis, bikes, fishing poles and boats – but he has never seen one that carries a wheelbarrow.

A New Industry Takes Over

With the turn of the century a new industry enveloped Mazama – building vacation and retirement homes. They sprang up like mushrooms after a spring rain. The entire upper valley experienced a building boom, but nearly a third of the new construction was in Mazama. In the first five years of the decade more than 300 houses were built in the area from Winthrop through the upper valley. About 90 of those new homes were in Mazama. This is more than had been built in the previous 60 years, and while there are no records to prove the numbers, it may be more than had ever been built in Mazama.

The year 2000 was a boom year. Building permits were issued for 20 homes in Mazama while 53 were issued for the rest of the upper valley. Mazama kept up the pace and in 2005 the Okanogan County Building Department issued 14 permits in the first six months of the year – all for Mazama. People were having to postpone construction projects because they couldn't find a contractor.

Because much of the undeveloped private land in the upper valley was on the south side of the Methow River and was included in the Arrowleaf project, people looking to build in the upper valley bought parcels along Lost River Road on the north side of the river. Contractor rigs, concrete trucks and loads of lumber started rolling past the

Mazama Store 12 months of the year. They disappeared into the many private roads serviced by the main county road, and it seemed that anyone who wanted a job could find work on somebody's retirement dream home or vacation getaway.

Lost River had its first new business in decades when John Morgan, Barbara House and Liam Doyle opened their Lost River Winery.

The Lost River Winery

One of the new homes up Lost River Road was being built for John Morgan and his wife Barbara House, who in 1994 moved to the Methow from Bellingham. John was from the Seattle area, a graduate of the University of Washington and a bridge engineer. Barbara was a nurse.

John had become increasingly frustrated by the many requirements that had to be met to get bridges built. On a trip through the California wine country, he and Barbara were impressed by the work and lifestyle of people in the grape-growing and wine-making in-dustry. John had been a hobby winemaker for some years. He was interested in making wine for commercial sale and studied for three years at the Univer-sity of California at Davis. He quit his job and started the Lost River Winery in Mazama. The

John Morgan, left, presides over the winery's original tasting room at Lost River.

couple built a house and the first winery building in 2001, which gave Lost River it's first commercial enterprise since the mining days and Archie Green's sawmill.

Lost River Winery is a family business with John, Barbara and her son, Liam Doyle, all working in some aspect of what now includes a tasting room and storage and sales building in Winthrop in addition to the Lost River facility. John contracts for specific acres of grapes from locations he scouts in Walla Walla, the Yakima Valley and on the Wahluka Slope to get the fruit he needs for his various wines.

When plans for the Arrowleaf Resort died, the Trust for Public Land, a national non-profit conservation organization, negotiated to buy out the developers. They acquired about 1,000 acres of land worth millions of dollars.

Arrowleaf Fades Away

Although there were many factors at play, the final blow to dreams for the Arrowleaf Resort was the Washington State Department of Ecology's refusal to make a decision on the project's water rights. After years of study and negotiations, the developers still needed to be assured of water for the golf course that was to be built. Golf was an important element for the resort plan. So confident were the developers that they had ample and adequate existing water rights that the golf course was started and some of the fairways cleared.

Apparently the DOE would not make a decision on the authenticity of the claims one way or the other. The project water specialists and lawyers were confident that even if the DOE would not honor the rights, or refused to allow the water use, the project would prevail in an appeal to the courts. However, when the DOE refused to make any decision, there was nothing to appeal, making resolution impossible.

This was the last straw for the Merrill Company. Their backup position was to give up on the golf course and resort and simply subdivide the property into about 70 home sites, sell them off and recapture their costs. A number of people in the community feared the impact of the l,000-acre subdivision that could result from the liquidation of all the proposed resort real estate.

In one of the many negotiations between Merrill and the Methow Valley Citizens

Council, Merrill had agreed to give the MVCC the right to purchase the land if the resort was not built. In return, the MVCC agreed not to oppose a smaller resort. The MVCC appealed Merrill's plans anyway, but Merrill kept its part of the bargain and offered the land to the citizens council. Suddenly, the MVCC needed money and expertise. Craig Lee, from the Northwest office of the Trust for Public Land, was called in by the MVCC to facilitate disposition of the agreement.

The Trust for Public Land Arrives

The Trust for Public Land is a national, non-profit conservation organization that strives to "... conserve land for people to enjoy as parks, gardens, and other natural places, ensuring livable communities for generations to come."

Negotiations went on for months, deadlines for action and compliance came and went. The TPL was dealing not only with the Merrill Company, but with Seattle members of Friends of the Methow, and the very diverse MVCC.

There were numerous factions and all wanted some part of the pie. The Methow Valley Sport Trails Association, which maintains miles of the valley's most popular and scenic recreational trails, wanted continued access to the trails that crossed some of the 1,000 acres of land involved in the dispute. Environmental activists were working to prevent any activity they felt might endanger their particular interests. There were real estate professionals at the Trust for Public Land who needed to sell land and raise money to buy out Merrill. They had to be sure they had a product that was not too restricted to sell. Despite the sometimes conflicting interests, TPL was able to forge a compromise deal. But they also had to put together the financing, which proved a bit more challenging than anticipated.

On January 9, 2001, the *Wenatchee World* newspaper had a front page story headlined, "Methow Land Deal is Final, Conservationists hail closure of $15 million deal to protect Early Winters site." Craig Lee told the newspaper that three Seattle area buyers had bought parcels. Two more buyers were needed, plus conservation rights were to

The Trust for Public Land sold five large parcels of land that became a new gated community at Early Winters with conservation easements and public access to the groomed cross-country ski trail system.

be sold to the State Department of Fish and Wildlife and the Bonneville Power Administration. He also said that the TPL had borrowed money to complete the deal and wanted to quickly find buyers for the remaining parcels. The story said, "local residents greeted the news with mixed reaction."

The environmental community was very happy. Newspapers from afar published stories. The *Oregonian*, in Portland, carried the headline, "Methow Land Use Battle Ends, area wildlife will be protected." Stories told of saving 365 acres of old growth timber and habitat for endangered species including grizzly bears, wolves, Northern spotted owls, Chinook salmon and Tailed frogs. In the *Oregonian's* story, Lee explained that the area was one of the largest undeveloped and unprotected riparian areas in Washington state. The conservation story was dramatic. It helped attract buyers as well as grants and government aid to finance the plan.

 Several purchase price figures were quoted. The TPL estimated that by the time the costs of building roads, putting in underground power and paying for administration were added, the price tag would be about $18 million.

The TPL plan included pre-selling the three parcels at $2-3 million each and obtaining a $1.3 million grant from Seattle billionaire Paul Allen. Two additional parcels were to be sold for a total of $5-6 million. The balance needed was to be borrowed from the Bullitt, Gordon Lovejoy and Kongsgaard-Goldman foundations and a TPL revolving fund. The loans were to be repaid by getting grants and funds for conservation easements from the U.S. Forest Service, the Bonneville Power Administration and Washington State.

 After the publicity and celebrations settled down, questions were loudly raised in some quarters of Mazama. Would the new neighbors be as generous as Merrill and the Arrowleaf project developers had been? For example, to attract local favor, Merrill had contributed tens of thousands of dollars to the community for everything from kids' baseball to the summer music festival and environmental causes. They also had allowed hikers and bikers to use trails on the old Calloway Cassal homestead and the public had been welcome to picnic in the fields where cattle once grazed.

From the county's perspective there was concern about removing so much land from the tax rolls, compared with the tax income a resort would have generated. Some valley people felt no resort meant no economic generator, and no long-term jobs.

 One of the TPL funding source targets was the Bonneville Power Administration, which grants millions of dollars annually for improving fish habitat as mitigation for its hydro operations. TPL was hoping for a $3 million grant based on the conservation plan's value to the habitat of fish and other endangered species.

That argument agitated some of the valley old-timers and more conservative citizens, who told the BPA the TPL claims were a major overstatement of reality. They allowed as how it was a pretty place, but pointed out that it had been extensively logged, farmed, grazed and irrigated for most of the last 100 years and that it was just like much of the property in the Methow watershed. They also said that the land was a few hundred feet from a 400-lot subdivision and dozens of vacation homes. And they claimed that the river that runs next to the property is not prime habitat for Spring Chinook because it goes completely dry four out of five years.

Ken Sletten

A prominent player in the group concerned about using taxpayer funds for the conservation buyout was a Mazama wanna-be who had started building a home on Wolf Creek Road in the Lucky Jim area in 1992.

Ken grew up on a dryland wheat farm near Souris, North Dakota, earned a degree in electrical engineering, then came to the west coast and got a job with the U.S. Navy as a civilian engineer.

A longtime whitewater river runner, Ken discovered the Methow Valley in the early 1980s, was attracted by the possibility of a ski area and decided that it would be his home. This created considerable inconvenience because his job was in Keyport, Washington, at the Naval Undersea Warfare Torpedo Center, where he was a software engineer.

Despite the distance, he threw himself into Mazama activities and politics. He became precinct committeeman for the Republican Party. He researched the finances and activities of the buyout group and sent bulletins and e-mails to anyone interested.

Ken thought that if individuals and foundations saw fit to fund the buyout, that was fine, but taxpayers should not have to pay. He was particularly concerned by what he saw as party politics at work in support of using public funds to repay the financiers of a private buyout scheme.

The BPA decided not to fund the project. At that point, Ken felt he had done his job by keeping people informed. He went back to his multi-year house-building project but continued to be vigilant in informing the citizenry when he spotted what he thought were government agency abuses.

In the end, after many sleepless nights for the TPL's Craig Lee, and much political maneuvering, Lee announced that all of the loans and guarantees had been paid back

Part-time valley resident Ken Sletten was not pleased about how taxpayer dollars were being spent and became a citizen watchdog.

with interest. The U.S. Forest Service ended up buying a big piece of land, west of McGee Creek; the State Department of Fish and Wildlife paid for conservation easements donated by the landowners, and a million dollars or so was paid by the Washington State Wildlife and Recreation Fund.

Both sides of the debate were perhaps right. It was a partial taxpayer bailout for a few million dollars, but not the full amount of the project. One could argue that the protection of potential habitat and the public access to spectacular ski trails was worth the public expense. The critics argue that millions in public funds to protect the privacy of four wealthy estates and a river that is dry much of the year is a questionable expense.

The Methow Conservancy's Mazama Roots

For nearly 100 years the goals and aspirations of most in the Methow Valley, as well as the local government, was to grow the community, open the land to production, attract and invite business and industry, create jobs and improve the standard of living.

During and after World War II this was a difficult assignment. There just wasn't much going on in the upper Methow except some logging. The mining era was over, agriculture was marginal and the 1968 freeze eliminated many of the orchards. Making a decent living in the upper Methow was difficult, if not impossible.

The construction and opening of the North Cascade Highway in 1972 generally was considered a glimmer of hope for the valley economy and was partial justification for the millions of tax dollars spent by the federal government for construction.

With a highway to get here, and the possibility of resorts, or at least a ski area, a new wave of people arrived in the valley. Their goals and aspirations were somewhat different from those of the earlier settlers. Some were drawn by potential development or dreamed of building a business, but many came with an equal desire to preserve what they had discovered. They found a beautiful place and wanted to keep it just like the day they arrived.

One of the organizations formed to help "save the Methow" was the Methow Conservancy. Today's conservancy has great support and financial aid from absentee landowners and people new to the valley, but it's origins are very local.

The Burkhart family moved to Mazama in the mid-1950s and started ranching. The family of four children, three girls and one boy, were completely immersed in agriculture. They raised cows, struggled to grow hay in Mazama's rocky soil and farmed hundreds of acres of the Big Valley Ranch for many years. They didn't have a "side job" such as working at the mill or in the mines, as was the norm for Mazama people.

The youngest in the family was Delene, born in the mid-1960s. She grew up with all the agricultural traditions, including horses, cows, 4-H projects, big gardens and hard work. Being the youngest she felt she had to do all the boring work, like changing sprinklers. But she grew up with an appreciation for ranch life. After finishing school, she returned to Mazama, which was not the norm for young people at that time.

Her sisters left the valley after school to find work. Her brother Aaron Lee stayed in Mazama to help run the farm. He also started a packing/outfitting business. Delene and her brother were among the very few kids from Mazama of their entire generation who were able to stay in the valley.

Delene managed the Mazama Country Inn for a period, and in the early 1990s got into the real estate business. She married Bob Monetta, who had come to the valley during the ski resort boom time. With perfect timing, they bought the real estate firm where Delene worked. Valley real estate was hot. Their business was quite successful and that could have been the end of a happy story.

But Delene was concerned about what was happening to the land, the ranches, the open space and lifestyle she had known growing up. So she and like-minded friends, including Jo Ruoss, Ardis Bynum and Jay Lucas formed the Methow Land Trust. With the help of the Methow Institite Foundation, a group started by John Hayes for dealing with the trail system, they set up a tax-exempt corporation to help preserve agricultural land and open space. The objective was to offer alternatives to subdividing land that could protect the valley's rural character and be tax-deductible without relying on government programs, buyouts or other forms of outside support.

They got grants from the Kongsgaard-Goldman and Wilburforce foundations in Seattle, plus $70,000 from the Merrill Company. The Methow Land Trust later became the Methow Conservancy, and enlarged its board of directors to reflect a broader approach to conservation. The Conservancy was off and running. There were contributions from many individuals as well, and by the middle of the first decade of the 21st century, the organization could point to a number of successes.

One huge accomplishment was the Conservancy's facilitation of the purchase of the field at the corner of Highway 20 and Lost River Road. The Mazama Planning Committee had long wanted to preserve this open field and vista of the mountains, but the land was zoned for commercial development. When Ben Goetter and his wife, Kathryn Hinch, purchased this property and showed an interest in its preservation, the Methow Conservancy helped it happen.

Like many who have come from far away to settle in Mazama and leave their mark, Ben came from Birmingham, Alabama. He came by way of Seattle, where he came looking for a job with Microsoft in 1985. He got a job there, as did Kathryn. They worked as programmers in networking. They found the Methow Valley while vacationing at Sun Mountain in 1992, and began looking for property for retirement and vacation. They found their dream site a few miles west of Mazama on the Lost River Road.

They were concerned about the rapid rate of growth in the area and "didn't want it to grow to look like Ketchum, Idaho." They decided to do something and went to the Conservancy for assistance in finding what were considered the most important properties to "save" or preserve.

The "Mazama corners" were reported to be very important and possible to save because they were still in one ownership. They were zoned commercial and had been advertised and promoted for future business development. At one time there was a large sign declaring it the site of the future "Mazama Village." After a few months, nighttime pranksters painted out the letter "V" in Village and replaced it with a "P." Some months later, someone sawed through the wooden supports so the sign collapsed. This demonstrated the definite difference of opinion about land uses in Mazama. The land sat idle for years but it was very valuable because of its location and zoning.

Ben didn't want a strip mall in Mazama and here was a chance to help prevent one. Microsoft was at its peak in 1999 and Ben had participated in the company's generous employee stock option plan. As the stock kept climbing and splitting, Ben felt he and Kathryn could afford to do something big. With the advantage of a good tax benefit, they could preserve this field by buying it and putting it into a conservancy.

They bought the field and several adjoining lots, some of which were part of the Mazama Pines subdivision, for about $850,000. They put an easement on the field for agricultural use only and placed it in a conservancy trust.

At one point Ben's plan was to build a restaurant/bar on the adjoining lot, which was also zoned commercial, in hopes of earning enough to pay the taxes and maintenance on the property. Plans were drawn and the long approval process undertaken, but after many months of effort he could not get a permit for commercial water use. As bizarre as this "environmental" regulation was, Ben felt there was no appeal or resolution possible, so he sold the field and some adjoining property. The new owner built a large barn in the field and a big home on the adjoining lot. However, the field still is preserved as open space in agricultural production.

By the time all of the buying, selling and tax benefits were computed, Ben concluded that his contribution to saving the Methow and the character of Mazama cost him about $500,000.

Meanwhile, Jim Fisher, a local real estate broker who owned the land across the road from Ben and Kathryn's field, felt people driving along Highway 20 needed to see a sign that told them they were in Mazama. The Mazama Community Club took on the project by recycling a sign from the Early Winters Cabins and having local artist and sign maker Eric Burr show pictorially that hiking, biking and skiing were activities happening in this part of the valley. Jim granted permission to erect the new sign on his property. Even this project drew scoffs from those who saw it as undesirable boosterism.

Changes at an Old Homestead

Michal Friedrich, a Seattle dentist originally from Gdansk, Poland, is making dramatic changes on the old George Lintzmeyer homestead, which he now owns.

The place has had several owners and uses over the years. The Rocking Horse Ranch, started and operated by Shiril Cairns until her death in 1998, is probably the best known recent use of the land. After Shiril died, one of her daughters, Meghan Sullivan, and Meghan's husband Dave ran the place for awhile before it was sold. They then started the Rocking Horse Bakery in downtown Winthrop.

Michal put in a soccer field and built an all-steel house that has won notoriety and awards in architectural circles from Seattle to New York. He says he always wanted to live in a tree house, so he built his version in steel. Now he's restoring the old homestead house, barn and outbuildings, keeping their exterior appearance intact by recycling the old boards and siding – an effort appreciated by locals.

The old barn will be used for his Methow Springs bottled water business, which he bought from Okanogan County Commissioner Bud Hover, who started the enterprise at his place in the Wolf Creek area. And Michal is installing new structures in the former campground.

Michal Friedrich, a Seattle dentist and native of Poland, purchased the Rocking Horse Ranch. It is now Wesola Polana, Polish for "Happy Valley."

A new steel house is among the many changes Michal Friedrich has made at the old Rocking Horse Ranch.

The Seattle dentist discovered and fell in love with the Methow Valley in 1997 while attending a friend's wedding at Sun Mountain Lodge. And now that he owns a piece of paradise, he's renamed his spread Wesola Polana, which means Happy Valley in Polish.

The Fish-saving Controversy

After decades of controversy elsewhere over fishing rights among commercial fisherman, Indian tribes, sports anglers, government bureaucrats and environmentalists, the issue struck in Mazama. In the 1990s, and certainly by 2000, there were many fewer salmon spawning in Early Winters Creek and the upper Methow River. When the Spring Chinook salmon was listed as an endangered species by the National Marine Fisheries Service, it had a profound effect on Mazama.

Who is responsible for the decline of fish remains controversial, but a group of very aggressive bureaucrats decided that the Methow Valley should be the focus of an attempt to reverse the situation. All fishing above the Weeman Bridge was prohibited and all irrigation ditches in the upper Methow with a source on U.S. Forest Service land were either shut off or restricted from use except at times of high water. Under threat of severe penalties for non-compliance, ditches and waterways that flowed freely for many decades dried up. The green belts with bird and wildlife habitat created by leaky ditches started to turn brown and die. Some areas were affected more than others as the number of people farming steadily declined.

The Early Winters Ditch was the largest in the Mazama area, and of the original 10 to 15 farms that it served, only five were still irrigating land. However, the ditch association had approximately 40 members who used the waterway as an important amenity to their yard or property.

Negotiations were bitter, especially with the National Marine Fisheries Service. Lawsuits ensued with no real resolution. However, both state and federal funds were made available to mitigate some of the problems. Wells were drilled to provide irrigation water when the ditch was shut off. Water was put in closed pipes to prevent leakage and to preserve water.

At a cost of more than $200,000, the state Department of Fish and Wildlife replaced the fish screen to prevent fish from entering the ditch system from Early Winters Creek. The explanation was that although the existing screen was operational, the new screen was built at a slight angle, and it would tend to deflect small fish easier should they come in contact with it.

All this activity seemed to calm most Mazama people, but they still were puzzled by all the hullabaloo about the water level in a river that goes dry naturally in four out of five winters.

A New Plan for the Freestone Inn

In 2006, a group headed by Andy Norris, who helped plan Arrowleaf Resort while working for the Lowe Co., returned to Mazama with a new plan for the Freestone Inn and Wilson Ranch. The idea was to convert the inn and cabins to residential condominiums with fractional ownership, a concept that has been quite successful in other places. The plan included changes and upgrades; for example, the addition of a spa/fitness/wellness facility. However, by early 2008 that plan appeared to be going nowhere.

Mining Interests Return – Again

As this book goes to press the price of gold and copper stand at record highs. So perhaps it is not surprising that a recent issue of the *Methow Valley News* published a story saying that the Pacific Copper Corporation of Reno, Nevada, paid $500,000 for 114 claims above Mazama in 2006. The claims are 1,200 feet above the valley floor between Flag Mountain and Goat Peak. The company was said to be waiting for test results it hopes will verify historic ore samples.

How these and other evolving visions for recreation and mining and their potential tugs-of-war will fare is anyone's guess. What can be said is that Mazama still is a darned pretty place with a whole lot of nice people attempting to live their dreams.

Author's Biography

Doug Devin, a native of Seattle, served a tour in the U.S. Marine Corps before being graduated from the University of Washington in 1951 with a degree in economics and business. For three years, he worked for the Central Intelligence Agency in Europe, where he met his future wife Grace, a fellow employee. They were married in Salzburg, Austria.

For most of his urban life Doug was in some form of the ski business as an instructor, a ski shop owner, equipment importer and sales representative. He also was active in the printing industry and at one time was president of Bank Check Supply Co., a specialty firm that served Northwest banks.

Doug Devin

The Devin family started vacationing in the Methow Valley in the 1950s, bought land in the '60s and moved here full time in the late '70s. They were skiers all. Children Steve and Betsy Devin raced for the U.S. National Ski Team. Their dad thought he was moving here to help build a ski hill.

He was appointed to and chaired Okanogan County's original Methow Valley Land Use Advisory Committee in the early 1970s. That group developed the first comprehensive plan and zoning ordinance for the Methow Valley. He continues to serve on the Mazama Advisory Committee, an offshoot of the original group, which is focused on that portion of the valley stretching from Wolf Creek to Lost River.

The Devins started farming in the early 1980s. When Steve returned from college, he joined his parents in running the last cattle ranch in Mazama at the family farm on Little Boulder Creek. Growth and development in Mazama eventually made cattle impractical and most of the cattle were sold in 2003.

Grace died in 2001. Doug continues to travel, ski and raise and sell hay with his son. Steve and his wife Kristin also own the Mazama Ranch House tourist accommodations, among other enterprises. Betsy Devin-Smith is a veterinarian and owner of Winthrop Veterinary Services in Winthrop and together with her husband Skip and son Casey raises sheep and sells lamb.

The entire family continues to support numerous youth activities and the Methow Valley Ski Team.

Credits/Sources

Dozens of sources were consulted as this book was compiled. The oral and written recollections of longtime residents were especially valuable, although the author is grateful to all the sources listed here. This book would not have been possible without these individuals or the material collected from publications, museums and libraries. Any omission of individuals or events that should have been included in this history is strictly unintentional. Special thanks for guidance go to Sally Portman, author of *The Smiling Country* and to my late wife Grace for her invaluable assistance and encouragement.

Individual Contributors

Ella Black, Jerry Blann, Harold Bowers, Ardis Bynum, Bob Cram, Hank Dammann, Grace Devin, Stan Dick, Elinore Drake, Barbara Duffy, Jim Fisher, Darrell Ford, Walt Foster, Michael Friedrich, Barry George, Ben Goetter, Sandy Haase, Leslie Thompson Hall, John Hayes, Harold and Tina Heath, Kathryn Hinch, Francis and Jess Hintz, Hazel Hollaway, Chuck Hotchkiss, Doris and Roy Kumm, Bill Laney, Jay Lucas, Mary Milka, Laura Mueggler McCabe, Cathy McCauley, Delene Burkhart Monetta, Charlene Welch Monger, John Morgan, Della Northcott, Vernon Overturf, Larry Patterson, Bill and Vi Pederson, Randy Picklesimer, Bill Pope, Don and Sally Portman, Dick and Sue Roberts, Eric Sanford, Don and Dorothy Shafer, Bob and Maryanne Sitts, Bud Short, Ken Sletten, Bill and Martha Stewart, Wally Stewart, George Turner, Bill Wehmeyer, Mabel Wehmeyer, Gordon Welch, Elsie Wilson, Charlie Wright.

Diaries, books, newspapers and periodicals

The unpublished diaries of Zora Ballard, Ethel Hollaway and John McKinney.

High Hopes and Deep Snows by Marcy Stamper; *Late Frontier, A History of Okanogan County, Washington* by Bruce A. Wilson; *Methow Valley Pioneers* compiled by Dale Dibble; *The Smiling Country* by Sally Portman.

Omak Chronicle, Oregonian (Portland), *Methow Valley Journal, Methow Valley News, Seattle Times, Seattle Weekly, Wenatchee World.*

Northwest Discovery, Vol. 4, June 1983
Okanogan County Heritage

Libraries, museums and other sources

Okanogan County Assessor's Office, Okanogan County Building Department, Okanogan County Historical Society, Shafer Historical Museum, Transamerica Title, U.S. Forest Service-Winthrop District Office, University of Washington Libraries, Washington State Historical Society.

Photo Credits/Sources

Betsy Devin: Page 131.

Bill Devin: Page 20.

Doug Devin: Front cover; pages 5, 9-10, 17-22, 25-26, 28, 33-34, 36, 50, 67, 72-73, 91, 102, 108, 110, 112-114, 116, 119-120, 122, 128, 134-135, 146, 148-150, 157, 159-165, 167, 170-171.

Grace Devin: Page 173

Elinore Kent Drake: Pages 9, 93.

Roy Goodall: Page 153.

Ferd Haase: Page 92.

Martha Bertram Heaton: Page 14.

Cathy McCauley: Page 76.

Northwest Discovery: Page 8.

Okanogan County Historical Society: Front cover, pages 43, 61-63, 65, 107.

Omak Chronicle: Page 104.

Greydon Patterson: Front cover, page 86.

Pete Peters: Page 24.

Josef Scaylea: Page 111.

Shafer Historical Museum: Pages 6, 8, 10-11, 15, 25, 31, 36, 45, 47, 54-56, 58-59, 69, 74, 77, 79, 90, 96, 100.

Sloane family: Page 81.

Bud Short: Back cover, pages 13, 26-27, 60, 70, 88-89, 94.

Bob Spiwak: Pages 12, 117.

Stookey family: Page 32.

Washington State Historical Society: Bottom photo, page 11.

Dick Webb: Pages 106, 124.

Bill Wehmeyer: Pages 20, 35, 92-93, 95.

Wehmeyer family: Pages 35, 71-72.

Elsie Wilson: Page 115.

Map Credits

Eric Burr: Page 4.

Sally Ranzau: Pages 2, 7, 16, 23, 30.

Bill Tackman: Page 44.

Index